Dragonfly-Friendly Gardening

IN THE MOMENT

Ruary Mackenzie Dodds
with
Kari de Koenigswarter

Published by
Saraband
3 Clairmont Gardens,
Glasgow, G3 7LW

www.saraband.net

ISBN: 9781916812123

*In common with several organisations including the
British Dragonfly Society, for clarity we have used
upper-case initial letters when giving the common
names for the dragonfly and damselfly species ('Ruddy
Darter', etc) and plants whenever particular species
are referred to throughout this book.*

Printed and bound in Great Britain by
Clays Ltd, Elcograf S.p.A.

10 9 8 7 6 5 4 3 2 1

Contents

To our family

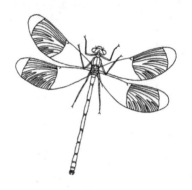

"The beginning of autumn,
Decided
By the red dragon-fly."

—Shirao

My Dragonflies

Of all the insects in the skies
the brightest are my dragonflies.
My dragonflies are stained-glass men
who loop and turn and loop again.
On crystal wings they catch the light,
like neon shards in jump-jet flight.

The sun and wind combine to make
a million diamonds on the lake.
Ripple-flash echoes on the mill —
My dragonflies are brighter still.

Ruary Mackenzie Dodds

Dragonfly Gone

Past my head, it flitters in the air
like pages fluttered in the wind.
I turn and watch it hover by a branch;
it glows, a jewelled flickering snitch

It freezes on a trinity of leaves.
I go too close, too fast.
Gone. I gasp at gone-ness.

It's back, as if it never moved;
its lattice wings hold stained-glass glints;
Its long slim abdomen pulsates,
a blue and green kaleidochrome.
Its jointed leg, claw-tipped, swings up
to scrape across it compound eyes.
Its head slews robot-like at prey
Those eyes are bulging honeycombs

Gone. In a shuddering of wings.

Ruary Mackenzie Dodds

Silent Noon

Your hands lie open in the long fresh grass,—
The finger-points look through like rosy blooms:
Your eyes smile peace. The pasture gleams and
glooms
'Neath billowing skies that scatter and amass.
All round our nest, far as the eye can pass,
Are golden kingcup fields with silver edge
Where the cow-parsley skirts the
hawthorn-hedge.
'Tis visible silence, still as the hour-glass.

Deep in the sun-searched growths the dragon-fly
Hangs like a blue thread loosened from the sky:
—So this wing'd hour is dropt to us from above.
Oh! clasp we to our hearts, for deathless dower,
This close-companioned inarticulate hour
When twofold silence was the song of love.

Dante Gabriel Rossetti,
from *The House of Life*

Prologue

I'm standing on the towpath of the Grand Union Canal at Denham, holding a camera, alone in the sunshine, trying to relax from my super-pressurized job in Kensington. I'm here to get a dose of fresh air, soak up the calm, maybe take a few arty photographs.

A dragonfly lands on my shirt, and three things happen, lightning fast. *One*: I don't really like insects, but I'm completely comfortable with this amber-black thing sitting above my heart. *Two*: I actually look at a dragonfly, properly, for the first time in my life. It's beautiful. I feel a strange sense of wonder. *Three*: the dragonfly says, 'Why not photograph dragonflies?' and vanishes in a whirr of wings.

I'm left with the oddest feeling, much stronger than just an idea about photography. It's … I don't know. Something a bit like a *déjà-vu*, but not. An intuition?

I live in central London but I'm always seeking out quiet places: parks, woodlands and especially canals. Canals are like veins of peace; glass-smooth and thin, slipping discreetly past noisy factories and under busy streets. Bits are ugly, bits are dangerous, but the part I'm in right now threads through a mile-long fragment of countryside somehow left behind in the middle of all the bricks and concrete.

The Grand Union at Denham is bounded to the south by the roar of the M40, and to the north by trains heading to High Wycombe and beyond. It's a little area of leafy, watery quiet. The banks of the canal are lined with old oaks. Keeping company with the canal is the River Colne, and there are several broad gravel pits, worked out now and filled with water. It's the combination of canal, river and placid lakes that makes the place so attractive.

Anyway, I started to photograph dragonflies. Things have changed a bit since 1985. I'd have a digital camera now, and I wouldn't have to wait for prints to come back, but I'd still need a sunny day, a great deal of patience, and clothes I didn't mind getting seriously dirty. I'd still have to be ready to crawl and I'd probably end up with wet shoes.

After many attempts, the first successful picture I got was of a damselfly, not a dragonfly. When I took the photo I didn't know the difference between the two, but now I do: when it lands, if it leaves its wings out flat like an aeroplane, it's a dragonfly. If it folds them neatly back, along what I kept calling its fuselage until I learned it's the abdomen, it's a damselfly. Of course, as with most simple definitions there are exceptions, but just being aware of that difference means I already know more about Odonata than 99.9% of the world's population. Odonata is the proper name for the Order that includes both dragonflies and damselflies.

Kari, my partner (we're married now), got that first success. She didn't actually do any crawling or camera stuff, but her hawk-eyes spotted a tiny blue triangle in the grass. We were wandering through a field close to the canal later that summer. It had begun to cloud over. We'd decided we were out of luck when suddenly Kari pointed. I dropped to my knees and crept forward, warily as a cat. Into the viewfinder came an insect the colour of lapis lazuli, half of each elegant wing stained a deeper blue. I was transfixed. I've used that picture of a Banded Demoiselle (*Calopteryx splendens*, its Sunday name) again and again, on interpretation boards and in talks. Every time I see it, I feel the sense of wonder and victory – and something else, something hard to define – that shot through me on that quiet morning. Did I really take that in Denham, Middlesex? Did we only have to take the Central Line to West Ruislip then walk a bit? Not have to trek into the Brazilian jungle?

Hawk-Eye Kari had spent ten years of her adult life in New York. Like me, she wasn't interested in insects, but, almost as soon as I got the dragonfly-photography bug she showed an extraordinary ability to spot them. Genetic maybe; her grandfather, Charles Rothschild, was a pioneer of nature conservation, her mother Pannonica was named after a moth, and her Aunt Miriam was one of the world's leading authorities on fleas.

I never knew Charles Rothschild; he died in 1923. But I knew Nica and Miriam well. I met Miriam first. She wasn't exactly an ordinary person, and her home at Ashton Wold wasn't an ordinary house. They've gone now. I still go back, but only in my head. And in my heart.

SATURDAY, MARCH 22ND, 1980: LONDON

(Five years earlier)

I don't feel very well, but I'm ignoring it. Kari and I are in a little Citroën Dyane heading for Ashton Wold, on our way to see Kari's Aunt Miriam. I don't know much about her. Kari's very fond of her and wants us to meet. I'm told she's a flea expert, a serious fighter for wildflowers, and fellow of the Royal Society. Clearly not a lightweight.

The journey from London in the underpowered Dyane seems to take years but at about midday, we turn into a scene so twee it could be a film set:

thatched houses ring a village green, and at the top is a thatched pub, the Chequered Skipper. We've arrived? Wrong. We drive through the village to a lodge and a gate, beside which is a sign:

NOTICE:
NO PERSON IS PERMITTED TO TRESPASS
IN ASHTON IN SEARCH OF INSECTS.

We head up the private road. Later I hear this is called the 'drive', but that's a nonsense: it's nearly two miles of the bumpiest track imaginable, with potholes as long and as deep as trenches. The Citroën's suspension is built for French *pavé*, but as we crash and sway uphill I'm sure other cars soon fall to pieces under this treatment.

Eventually we reach Ashton Wold at the top. The track leads through lines of overgrown laurels and we run parallel to what is obviously the outside of a walled garden with potting sheds and a tired-looking Fergy tractor. Then we veer off round the service side of the house, so I can't work out the actual size of the place, but it's certainly big; and I like the look of its mullioned windows. As we swing round the bend I notice, in a copse beside the track, a moss-covered mountain of stone blocks topped by five upside-down cast iron baths, each with four fat little legs in the air.

We leave the car at one end of a small courtyard and go through a large white door at the other. The loud bang as it closes behind us echoes down the long, bare, whitewashed corridor ahead. At once we hear the sound of distant barking and a patter of many paws on parquet, and as we round the corner into an even longer much more elegant corridor, a pack of shelties – led by a small black mongrel – is hurtling towards us. I'm usually all right with dogs; not with this lot. They're after our ankles. On subsequent visits, I know to dodge smartly into the kitchen on the right and slam the door behind me, but not now.

'Come here!' yells an imperious female voice. 'Come here, I say.'

I look at Kari.

'She means the dogs,' says Kari, hopping sideways.

The seething, fanged mass of brown, white and black fur subsides and trots reluctantly back down the corridor into a distant set of rooms.

'Kari?' yells the voice again. 'Is that you?'

'Hello, Miriam,' Kari calls.

'With you in a minute. Help yourself to a drink. Sunday! Moonie! Come here!'

Kari and I walk into the library. As with the word 'drive', 'library' is a misnomer. It's a vast, bright, oak-panelled room, walled by ceiling-high bookshelves. At one end is a mighty mantelpiece with a Stanley Spencer painting of lilacs above it and a roaring fire below. Ranged round the fireplace are three massive sofas, each covered with a white throw and each showing signs of considerable doggy activity. At the other end of the room stands a concert-size Steinway and, under an enormous leadlight window, a long table piled high with brand new books: art, architecture, biographies, novels, scientific journals and Jewish politics. In the middle of the room is another table on which is a giant vase of (real) lilacs, and, nestled in the porchway looking out to the garden, another table with an array of drinks that would impress the most jaundiced of barmen. It includes vodka. I hover, uncertain. Kari taps the top of the vodka bottle.

'A big one,' she says. I obey and hand her a thumping glassful. She works at the same outfit as I do. She's Head of Marketing. I've watched her keep pace with very hard drinkers. Personally – and uncharacteristically – I settle for a glass of sherry.

I see the wellingtons first; they're white; I haven't seen any like that since my doctor father played Santa Claus at his local hospital in Lincolnshire. Then I see the dress, a beautifully cut billowy silk affair, white and violet. Then the scarf, also violet, tied so as to reveal sweeping curls of silver hair. A pale, almost translucent face; a sharp nose; high cheekbones; very piercing, fleeting eyes; and a sudden powerful presence.

'Hello,' says Miriam. 'Who are you?'

'I ...'

'Oh yes, I remember. Kari rang. Have a drink.'

'I have one, thank you. Would you ...?'

'No. Have you seen the snake's head fritillaries? On the tennis court. Go and look. Stay on the path. Lunch at one.'

We go out through the garden door and down pale spacious limestone steps to a terrace, then down more steps to another terrace and, brushing aside overgrown white lilacs, down yet more steps to the tennis court. It isn't a tennis court. I'm getting used to this. Yes, it has been, but now it's a yellow carpet of cowslips, dotted with purple fritillaries, with a tiny path weaving diagonally across it to a long rampart facing south. I leave Kari, bent over, gazing at the wildflowers, and tiptoe down the path. In the corner it leads to a hidden stairway. At the bottom is a wrought-iron gate to another overgrown garden. I can see a lily pond, and, on another terrace, a ruined thatched dovecote. There's the faintest air of sadness.

I turn and look back at the mansion. It's half-hidden by untrimmed trees, but, with its golden stonework and its mullions, it looks like a very large Edwardian version of a Sussex ironmaster's house, albeit strangely truncated. I discover later that, back in the Fifties, Miriam had all the roofs taken off, the entire middle floor removed, then the roofs put back on. As the masons took the stones down, they numbered each one and piled them all in that copse close to the house, then put the baths on top.

Kari calls me back and makes me crouch down to look at a snake's head fritillary. On its tiny, grape-red, bent-over bell of petals are minute brown flecks, repeating uniformly like a fleur-de-lis wallpaper pattern in miniature. We go back up to the house. As we walk back into the library, Miriam is on the phone.

'Well, you can tell the Lord Chancellor he'll have to cut his speech,' she says, and puts the phone down. I've heard her before, when she's rung Kari at our London flat. She never says goodbye. She swings round.

'Look here, there's no food. Margaret's not here. We'll have to go and scrounge.' The black mongrel is now gazing adoringly up at her. 'Come on, Sunday,' she says.

She leads the way into the dining room; another massive space, also oak-panelled, but a lighter shade, almost white. In the centre of the room is a grand table. I count fourteen

Chippendale chairs round it. In a long daffo-
dil-lined alcove by the window there's another
table. The smaller one can accommodate at
least a dozen, too, but it's set for three. There
are two sideboards: the nearest has ashets of
cold duck, cold roast beef, cold ham, smoked
mackerel, peas, tomatoes, salads of different
sorts, beetroot, potato salad, fennel and celery.
Miriam's idea of scrounging. On the far side-
board stands a small army of pickles, mayon-
naises, mustards and sauces. I glance at them
appreciatively.

'I hope you like quail's eggs,' says Miriam.
'Pour the wine, will you? None for me.'

The wine is a sparkling white, Pétillant
Deux-Sèvres.

'You'll never guess what Sid's done,' says
Miriam, turning to Kari, and so begins a long
conversation about the farm and the family. I
tuck into the eggs, and then the duck.

'Have some more, Ruary,' orders Miriam.

'I'm fine, thank you, that was delicious,' I say.

'Oh, go on,' she says testily. 'There's tons there.'

After the meal, we go upstairs, through the
spacious billiards room, to the bedroom we've
been allocated. Separate beds. It's crammed with
portraits and photographs of the family. I lie
down and begin to feel unwell again. I shouldn't

have eaten that vast lunch. It gets worse. I start to sweat. Eventually I tell Kari I won't be able to come down for tea.

'You've got to,' she says. 'Tea's important.'

'I can't. I'll throw up.'

'Miriam hates sick people.'

'Well, we'd better go back to London, while I can still drive. I'm really not right.'

'I'll go and tell her,' she says.

Kari goes downstairs, breaks the news, and an hour later, after I've built up strength, we repack and go out to the car. As we load our stuff, Miriam appears from the walled garden. She sees me, continues coming towards the house, but gives me a very wide berth, taking care to keep at least fifteen metres away.

SATURDAY, OCTOBER 11TH, 1980: ASHTON WOLD

After an enormous lunch – roast duck and Château La Cardonne claret – Kari and I go through that wrought-iron gate I saw on my first visit, past the lily pond, through another iron gate and into the deer-field. Under a dark sky, we're walking down to Ashton Water. I haven't been there before and we're with Kari's cousins – Miriam's children – Charlotte and Charles. They both have auburn hair, very bright against the greyness of the day. They have their own flats within the house, and Ashton is their home when they aren't working in London.

We head downhill through woodland trampled by deer to a lake that looks like something out of Africa: bare, muddy and pocked with thousands of hoof-marks. There's the Top Pond upstream of it with the same devastated look, and between them stands a small ten-sided building with a faded duck-egg blue door, the observation hut. The thatch is badly damaged. As well as a conical thatched roof, it has thatched walls and odd-shaped, many-paned broken windows on one side only, all looking out over the lake. I peer in through one of the jagged glass rectangles: nothing except a pile of hay, an empty bottle and a broken three-legged chair, lying sideways on a perfectly laid wooden floor that even through the dust and grime looks good enough to dance on.

The lake has two little islands and is surrounded by old willows, some so tall as to have dropped whole boughs that have fallen and reared up again as separate trees. The water is a flat brown. Even at that moment, as we walk round the margin of the lake, talking of nothing in particular, our voices echoing over the silent still surface, I have a strange feeling. This lake is calling to me.

From: *The Dragonfly Diaries*

First Principles

Why Dragonfly-Friendly Gardening?

Seven good reasons. You'll be creating a new and delightful dimension in your garden. You'll come across a new range of quietly colourful plants. You'll be providing a home for a species that lives in two worlds, the aquatic and the aerial. You'll find yourself discovering a whole new universe without leaving home. You'll have a great deal of interest and fun. You'll be getting quite a bit of exercise. And you'll be making a serious personal contribution to conservation.

What's So Special About Dragonflies?

They are the most amazing insects. If you take just a couple of moments really to look at a dragonfly, you'll see it's extraordinarily beautiful. What astonishing colours! You'll be looking at an adult, but in fact dragonflies spend most of their lives under water as larvae; a typical dragonfly can live two to three years under water before emerging to fly for about eight weeks. Once on the wing, their flight characteristics are phenomenal: they can cover 15 metres in less than a second, they can hover, spin on their own axis, fly backwards, and travel enormous distances. Each of their four wings can operate independently. They don't sting, they come in all sorts of colours, they have a fascinating life cycle – take a look at the diagram on pages 16–17 – and they eat insects that harm us, such as mosquitoes, gnats, midges and flies.

How Do I Become a Dragonfly-Friendly Gardener?

Where to start? Let me surprise you by suggesting that maybe the best way for a future DFG to begin is to take a sunny summer's day – and I do mean sunny – and leave home. Head for your favourite local water spot: that wildlife pond nearby, the little river, those fishing lakes, the sleepy canal …

First Principles

Take something to sit on – a stout shopping bag works for me – and plonk yourself down by the water's edge. And just watch. Be patient. If it's the right sort of habitat – it usually is, and I'll explain about that shortly – pretty soon you'll see some action. A little neon-blue damselfly fluttering in among the reeds; perhaps a Darter dragonfly perching, then zooming up to catch mosquitoes; or a big yellow-green Hawker dragonfly patrolling up and down. Or all three, and more. Why not try a couple of pictures with your phone or your camera? Wait till they land. If you move *very* slowly, you can go as close as you like. These are the beauties that can come to your garden.

When you're looking at a pond or body of water, there are some simple rules of thumb for knowing whether it's a good place for dragonflies, so before you leave your favourite water spot, ask yourself five questions:

- Is it getting plenty of sunshine on the water surface?

- Is the water fairly clear?

- Has it got surface-covering plants like water lilies?

- Has it got tall-stemmed plants like rushes, irises or reeds?

- Has it got water plants beneath the surface, plants that oxygenate the water?

LIFECYCLE OF THE DRAGONFLY

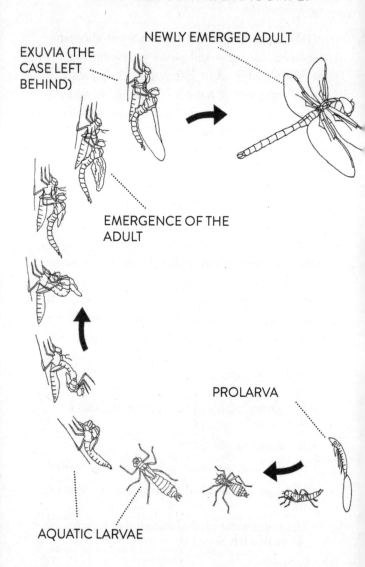

NEWLY EMERGED ADULT

EXUVIA (THE CASE LEFT BEHIND)

EMERGENCE OF THE ADULT

PROLARVA

AQUATIC LARVAE

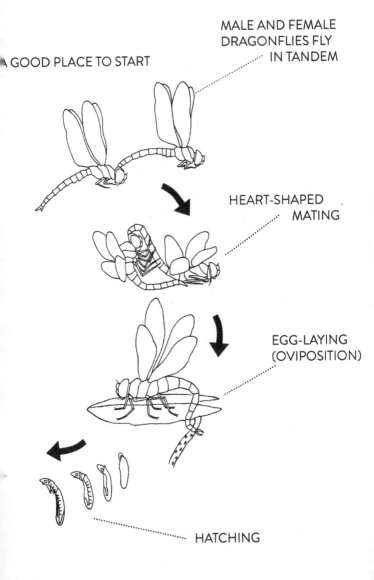

A GOOD PLACE TO START

MALE AND FEMALE
DRAGONFLIES FLY
IN TANDEM

HEART-SHAPED
MATING

EGG-LAYING
(OVIPOSITION)

HATCHING

Male and Female Dragonfly Fly in Tandem

The male finds a female and uses his claspers at the end of his abdomen to hold her by her head (dragonflies) or neck (damselflies) to form a tandem pair.

When They Mate They Form the Shape of a Heart:

They each curve their abdomen so that the end of the female's abdomen meets with the base of the male's in the so-called heart or wheel position. This can last from a few seconds to more than an hour depending on the species.

The Female Lays Her Eggs (Oviposition):

Some females lay eggs in plants in or near water; other species drop them directly into the water. Some will go right under the water to lay their eggs. The male often stays on guard to prevent any other male from mating with her.

Most Eggs Hatch in a Few Weeks

Most dragonflies lay eggs which will hatch within a few weeks. Some, however, lay eggs which will overwinter and not develop and hatch until the following spring.

A 'Teneral':The Newly Emerged Adult

The newly emerged dragonfly, called the 'teneral', is pale and soft. It will fly away from water to feed for several days. It will catch and eat small flying insects, using its bristly legs as a basket-like trap. When fully mature it will return to water to mate and oviposit (lay eggs).

Emergence of the Adult May Take 3 Hours, it is Very Vulnerable at this Time.

When it is ready the larva climbs out of the water for its final moult. It attaches itself by its claws to the stem of a plant or any other suitable surface, and splits the skin behind its head. The adult then slowly withdraws its body from the outer casing. Once this is done it pumps blood around the body, enlarging it, and expands the two pairs of transparent glistening wings. Emergence can take from 1 to 3 hours or more and usually occurs at night or in the morning. The case it leaves behind is called an 'exuvia'.

Dragonflies and Damselflies Can Spend Anything from 3 Months to Over 5 Years as Aquatic Larvae.

The tiny larvae grow and will shed their hard outer skin 11 to 15 times before they are ready to emerge. They often lie under silt or plant debris or hide in the leaves of submerged plants waiting for their prey to pass by. They shoot out their pincer like mouth parts and catch smaller aquatic animals.

If the answer is yes to all five of the questions on page 15, you can be pretty sure your chosen spot is good for dragonflies, and this of course will be what you, as a DFG, need to aim for in your pond. Big water spaces can accommodate some plants that might take over in your garden, so what you create at home won't be exactly the same as what you've just been looking at, but those five principles remain. Besides, great stretches of reeds and bulrushes are not especially interesting or colourful, and so one aim of this book is to make your pond more exciting. There'll be no need to worry about introducing dragonflies. Provided you take care of some simple rules, they'll come of their own accord.

Then ask yourself, do you really want to make a home for these amazing aerial acrobats? You have to be sure, because it's going to need work. If you already have a pond, you're halfway there, but if you haven't, well, a pond is what you need; and much of the enjoyment will be in the design and creation of your own water space. But whether you already have a pond or intend to make one, do bear in mind that it will need regular maintenance as the years go by.

I promise the rewards will be worth it. As a DFG, there'll be nothing quite like watching a Chaser dragonfly emerge from your pond, extract itself from its larval case, extend its wings and fly away; or seeing a Hawker dipping her abdomen in the water's edge to lay her eggs, setting another generation in train in your garden. And knowing you've been the one to help that happen. Alfred Lord Tennyson summed it up:

> *Today I saw the dragonfly*
> *Come from the wells where he did lie.*
> *An inner impulse rent the veil*
> *Of his old husk: from head to tail*
> *Came out clear plates of sapphire mail.*
> *He dried his wings: like gauze they grew;*
> *Thro' crofts and pastures wet with dew*
> *A living flash of light he flew.*

Making a home for dragonflies in your garden pond will do two things. First, it'll give you years of pleasure, not only from the dragonflies you attract, but also from all the other pond life that appears. Second, I'm serious when I say you really can claim to be making a genuine contribution to conservation. It's not generally known that huge amounts of dragonfly habitat have disappeared in the last 400 years. For example, in East Anglia in 1637 there were 3,380 square kilometres of wetland. If you're a dragonfly, wetland means home. By 1986 there were just 10 square kilometres left. If you think in acres, that's roughly 845,000 acres down to 2,500 acres. This is why I'm not in favour of peat-based compost, as it almost certainly comes from land that used to be dragonfly habitat.

Happily, organisations like the Wildlife Trusts, the National Trust, the Wildfowl & Wetlands Trust, the John Muir Trust and the RSPB are now all taking serious strides towards re-establishing large areas of wetland, but there's still a massive deficit. Think of all the thousands of farm ponds that have been grubbed out. So you really can help; you can tip the balance a little the other way.

Of course, with ponds, there are safety considerations. If you already have a pond, you'll be aware that toddlers need to be watched, or kept away with a small protective fence. You might consider a firm, wood-framed wire mesh cover when youngsters are to play in the garden unsupervised. A raised pond is another thought. Don't take risks. A wag once asked me whom I was protecting, the toddlers or the dragonflies. But a dragonfly pond needn't be deep. Even a couple of feet of water at the deepest point is fine, and a gentle gradient all round can work well too. Have a look at the diagram on pages 44–45.

First Principles

How Do I Identify the Dragonflies Visiting My Pond?

Did you take any photographs while you were at your favourite waterside spot? At some point, you'll be able to look back and know exactly what you saw that first day. It's just possible that you snapped a damselfly or dragonfly which may not visit your pond, because some species like only flowing water, whereas others like only still water. Many are quite happy with both. In any case, you'll get a good variety at your pond, and of course having such a pond is an ideal way of getting up to speed on your identification skills.

By the way, can I remind you of the difference between a dragonfly and a damselfly? It's easy. Wait until it lands: if it holds its wings out flat like a plane, it's a dragonfly. If it folds its wings flat, back along its fuselage-like abdomen, it's a damselfly. I've lost count of the times I've stuck my arms out to my sides – like a child playing planes – to indicate a dragonfly's wings in parked position, and then behind my back to indicate how a damselfly does it. There are, of course, exceptions, but that's a pretty reliable starting point.

Dragonfly-Friendly Gardening

Dragonflies are usually beefier, heftier insects than their smaller, more delicate damselfly cousins. Dragonflies generally have their eyes very close together whereas damselflies' eyes are widely separated. Both dragonflies and damselflies are sub-orders of the order Odonata, which means 'toothed ones' in Greek. They don't actually have teeth but they have pretty amazing mouthparts – more later – but, once you have a dragonfly pond and get more involved with dragonflies, you can think about calling yourself an odonatologist … if you dare. I tend not to; I usually stumble over its pronunciation.

A word of warning: the word 'dragonfly' is tricky as it's often used for the whole order, ie both dragonflies and damselflies. When Kari and I looked after a three-acre lake in Northamptonshire, I would proudly tell visitors that by fencing deer out and putting local native water plants in we had attracted seventeen species of dragonfly to the lake. In a sense I was cheating because I was lumping proper dragonflies and damselflies together. People often proudly tell me how many dragonfly species they have at their pond, and they're including damselflies in their total.

You may find yourself doing the same in due course. In my case, I also wasn't differentiating between species that actually decided to breed in the lake and ones that just happened to visit. In any case, from now on, unless I specifically say otherwise, I'll be using the word 'dragonfly' to include both sub-orders – in other words, both dragonflies and damselflies.

There's more help with identifying dragonflies in the 'Seeing What Comes' chapter (page 65).

On the following pages, you'll find a simple outline of a typical adult damselfly, outlines of two typical adult dragonflies, one large and one small.

On the pages after these (pages 29–31), you'll see outlines of the larvae.

What Equipment Do I Need to Be a DFG?

Damselflies will visit and sometimes breed in large, carefully planted water containers – even big old sinks (we have one in our garden). But, put simply, for most dragonflies you need a pond. I'll show you how to create one. If you've already got one, take a look at what I recommend; you might like to adjust yours to make it more attractive for dragonflies. Read on ...

Dragonfly-Friendly Gardening

TYPICAL LARGER DRAGONFLY

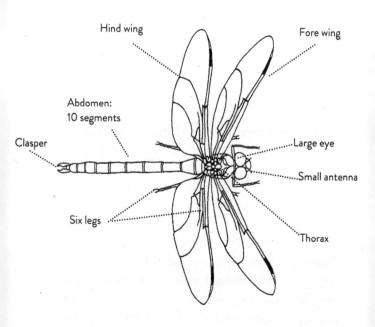

Hind wing

Fore wing

Abdomen:
10 segments

Clasper

Large eye

Small antenna

Six legs

Thorax

First Principles

TYPICAL SMALLER DRAGONFLY

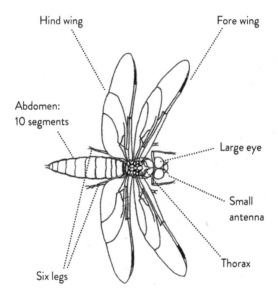

Hind wing

Fore wing

Abdomen:
10 segments

Large eye

Small
antenna

Thorax

Six legs

Dragonfly-Friendly Gardening

TYPICAL DAMSELFLY

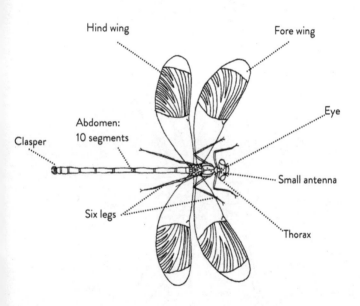

Hind wing

Fore wing

Eye

Abdomen:
10 segments

Clasper

Small antenna

Six legs

Thorax

LARGE DRAGONFLY LARVA

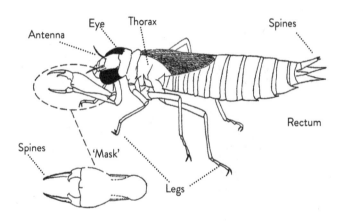

TYPICAL LARVAL SHAPES:
DRAGONFLIES

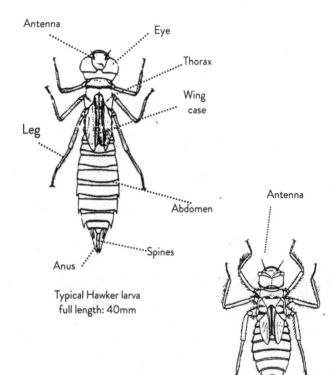

Antenna

Eye

Thorax

Wing case

Leg

Abdomen

Spines

Anus

Typical Hawker larva
full length: 40mm

Antenna

Typical Chaser larva
full length: 25mm

TYPICAL LARVAL SHAPES:
DAMSELFLIES

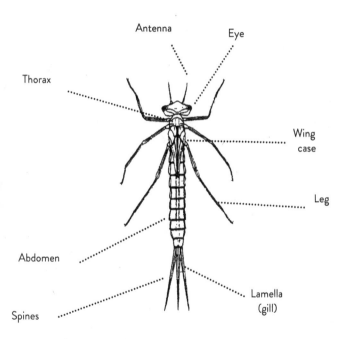

Antenna

Eye

Thorax

Wing case

Leg

Abdomen

Lamella (gill)

Spines

Typical damselfy larva
full length: 13mm

Why Write This Book?

Kari and I have been working with dragonflies ever since 1985. Up to that point we really hadn't had any contact with dragonflies. We weren't naturalists, we weren't entomological – we were busy working in London. But then a dragonfly landed on my shirt, and everything changed. I've written about it in *The Dragonfly Diaries* (Saraband, 2014; see the extract at the beginning of this book), but, in short, we ended up first running a Dragonfly Sanctuary, then the National Dragonfly Museum for seven years, then helping to organise the Dragonfly Centre at the National Trust's Wicken Fen Nature Reserve in Cambridgeshire. Aided by a truly fantastic bunch of loyal volunteers, we took thousands of people out into wetlands to show them dragonflies in action. We ran courses, dug ponds, manned stands at shows, and we've done lots of radio and TV work. Indeed, we've devoted a substantial part of our lives to dragonflies, and to getting the message across that dragonflies are fascinating, beautiful and in trouble ... and that you can help. Remember, every pond counts!

Preparing for Your Pond
and Creating it

If you already have a pond, please don't skip this chapter, as it may well stimulate you into carrying out just a few changes that will make all the difference for dragonflies. Take a look, for example, at what I say about water supply, and about maybe adding a boggy area to your pond. And, if you're starting from scratch, this is where you begin.

The carpenter's old adage 'Measure twice, cut once' is well worth bearing in mind; only of course with your pond it's a case of 'Measure twice, *dig* once'. But even before you begin your measuring, you'll need to work through two sets of criteria: what's best for you and your garden, and what's best for dragonflies.

I'm going to start with what's best for dragonflies, because I don't want you to decide on a plan for you and your garden, only to find I'd prefer you – ideally – to change it to fit dragonflies. What I suggest now will perhaps influence you to come up with a pond that dragonflies like, whilst at the same time creating something with which you yourself are really happy.

Where to Put the Pond

So far as dragonflies are concerned, it's best to decide about your pond when all the trees in your garden – and in those of neighbouring gardens – are in full leaf. Choose a spot that gets maximum sunshine. Dragonflies really operate best in sunny places, so the more sunshine on your future pond, the more dragonfly activity you'll get. Besides, leaf litter dropping into your pond can cause problems: you might be surprised to know that leaves from willow trees give off chemicals that may upset the water quality of your pond. Other trees to avoid close by are: horse chestnut, laburnum, rhododendron, yew, and *Prunus* species such as cherry. There's also the risk of tree roots disturbing your carefully laid pond liner.

I'm not suggesting that you set out your pond in the garden equivalent of a billiard table. Dragonfly ponds work best when protected from north and west winds. Trees set a little further away are very good windbreaks, as are bushes and hedges a little closer. I mention windbreaks because, during question-times in my talks, I'm often asked by people who don't have ponds why they sometimes find dragonflies whizzing around their back gardens. In return I ask the questioner whether her or his garden has a sheltered sunny space, to which the reply is invariably, 'Yes!' That's because dragonflies love to hunt for mosquitoes, gnats and midges in sheltered sunny spaces. So protecting your pond from the wind, especially from the north and west, is quite important, and it may also reduce evaporation.

At this point do make sure that what you have in mind isn't going to disturb any underground cables, conduits, water pipes and drains. Better to check now rather than get a nasty surprise later.

Water Supply

Good water quality is vital for dragonflies. They are very sensitive bio-indicators and a thriving population of dragonflies and damselflies at almost any wild water space is a simple way to know that the water quality is good.

So, right at the start of your planning, you need to think about the water supply to your pond. A hose from your kitchen or outside tap will do, but mains water does contain quite a few nutrients, and in certain conditions these can cause algal blooms and blanket weed growth. Some people are lucky enough to have a stream, free from agricultural run-off, or a supply from nearby hills, but for most of us, rainwater is the answer. If there's a way you can connect the water that comes off your roof with a pipe to your pond, maybe via water butt with a hose connection, that's much the best.

I mentioned a stream just then, and earlier I talked of dragonfly species that like flowing water. Of course it's great if you have a stream, as you can create the best of both worlds and have still water spaces and faster-flowing areas, but even if, like most of us, you don't have a stream, you can always consider making an artificial one. Garden centres can supply you with pre-formed fibreglass shapes, electric pumps, filters, cables and kits. You can even make fountains, waterfalls, concrete channels and interlinked pools, and there are excellent guides to help you with their construction, but again, for most of us, a simple pond is all we need. Running water won't make that much difference to the number of dragonfly species that come to your garden, and tiny damselfly larvae have been known to get trapped in the filters and pumps. If you do opt for running water, keep it gentle, as lilies are unhappy with too fast a flow.

No Fish

One thing to say right now: no fish. I do appreciate that people can derive huge pleasure from ornamental fish, so by all means have fish if you absolutely insist, but in that case you will have a fishpond with *some* wildlife, whereas if you don't put fish in, you'll have a *proper* wildlife pond with all the wonderful variety of species that arrive – and dragonflies will be part of that balanced habitat. Fish take over. So, on balance, please, no fish. And if you already have fish, might you have room for another, fish-free, pond? You wouldn't be the first …

Pond Size and Shape

You've thought about where best to put the pond, in a nice and sunny place. And you've considered the water supply. Now you need to think about the size of the pond. In short, the simple rule is: big is best, small is fine. A pond with a surface area of about 14 square metres is ideal, but something in the order of 3.75 square metres will do. Even a raised pond on a (strong!) balcony will attract dragonflies – not in huge numbers, but enough to be interesting.

When we had our three-acre lake, a visiting dragonfly professor remarked that the dragonflies would probably prefer the big lake to be divided into four ponds, because dragonflies really like lots of bankside margin. For most of us, the size of the pond will be dictated by the size of our gardens and the amount of space that gets sunshine. Any passing dragonfly will tell you that you need to plan the biggest pond that you can afford and that fits your garden!

If you've decided on a raised pond, you will of course have what we call 'cliff-sides', in other words your liner will rise vertically all round the edges. At the Argaty Red Kite Centre, near Doune in Scotland, there is such a pond. It's a magnet for dragonflies and for visitors. It is used regularly in the summer to show people dragonfly activity at close quarters, and there is usually plenty going on.

If you decide to go for a pre-formed pond, you'll find plenty of different shapes and sizes both on the Internet and at garden centres, and you'll have a fair amount of dragonfly activity, but you will also have 'cliff-sides'. I have yet to find a pre-formed pond with a gentle gradient.

But ideally dragonflies like gentle gradients, so if you have a choice, make sure you have a gradient, preferably in the northern and western ends of your pond. This provides gradual changes in water temperature, as the shallower the water, the warmer it becomes, and warmer temperatures can encourage larvae to emerge sooner. A

30cm-wide ledge, running round about 20cm below the water surface, will be very useful as it creates slightly different underwater habitats.

So those are the dragonflies' preferences. Do you think they match yours? I do hope so.

This brings us to the shape of the pond. It doesn't have to be fancy. A rough, slightly wiggly oval usually works, but there's no fixed rule. It's up to you, but you might consider two points. First, what about a small bog-garden at one end, maybe the northern end so that the gentle gradient I recommended merges into it? If your garden isn't level, choose the lowest end for your bog-garden. Either way, this will give you the chance to have a bigger variety of water-loving plants. It will add colour, too, and make a little extra habitat for dragonflies. Second, before you dig, don't forget about the possibility that you might want to extend your pond at some point, or create another close by. It's worth thinking about what you might like in years to come.

And something really important: think of how you're going to be able to reach parts of your pond, if necessary, once plants have grown up. Best of all, make sure you leave enough places for you just to sit and enjoy what goes on. Large stones to sit on, or an old bench will not only reward you, but they will also be very attractive to dragonflies; several species really like to bask and absorb the heat from warm stone and old grey wood.

Making plans

It's time to sketch out plans. The two key sketches will be:

- An aerial view of the proposed pond
- A cross-section

I've included an example of both as a guide (following pages).

In addition to a gradient, you will need to think about having different levels, and about the maximum depth you want. Dragonflies don't need more than about 60cm at the deepest point, although ponds over 20 square metres will need 75cm or more.

A trick for getting a clear picture of what the pond will look like is to measure out the ground area, drive in pegs at 30cm intervals and then lay an empty hose around it. You can then adjust the pegs until you're happy with the way it looks.

Remember that your pond needs to be level, so use the pegs, a plank and a spirit level to make sure. Leave the pegs and the hosepipe in place for a day or two, let your imagination run free, and allow yourself to feel absolutely confident that you're happy with what you're going to do. Once you're satisfied, fill a dry watering can with dry sand and pour the sand along the outline you have chosen.

Dragonfly-Friendly Gardening

AERIAL VIEW OF YOUR POND

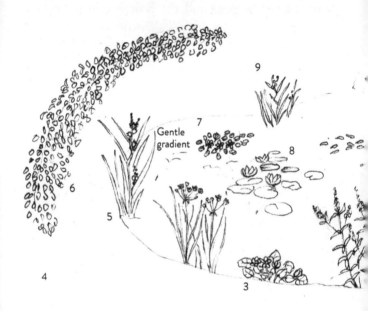

Gentle gradient

1	Yellow Flag Iris	*Iris pseudacorus*
2	Purple Loosestrife	*Lythrum salicaria*
3	Marsh Marigold	*Caltha palustris*
4	Flowering Rush	*Butomus umbellatus*
5	Branched Bur-reed	*Sparganium erectum*
6	Hedge	
7	Fringed Water Lily	*Nymphoides peltata*
8	White Water Lily	*Nymphaea alba*
9	Branched Bur-reed	*Sparganium erectum*
10	Amphibious Bistort also known as	*Persicaria amphibium*, *Polygonum amphibium*

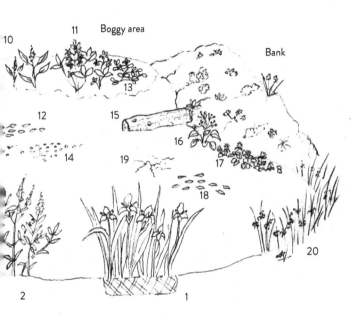

11 Bogbean   *Menyanthes trifoliata*
12 Broad-leaved Pondweed *Potamogeton natans*
13 Brooklime   *Veronica beccabunga*
14 Curled Pondweed   *Potamogeton crispus*
15 Log
16 Water Plantain   *Alisma plantago*
17 Water Mint   *Mentha aquatica*
18 Broad-leaved Pondweed *Potamogeton natans*
19 Hornwort   *Ceratophyllum demersum*
20 Soft Rush   *Juncus effusus*

A CROSS-SECTION OF YOUR POND

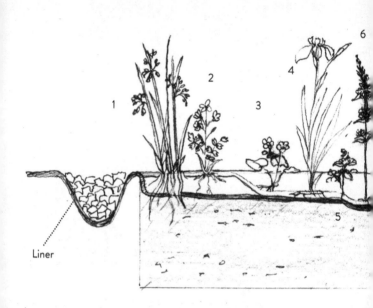

Liner

1	Soft Rush	*Juncus effusus*
2	Cuckoo Flower	*Cardamine pratensis*
3	Marsh Marigold	*Caltha palustris*
4	Yellow Flag Iris	*Iris pseudacorus*
5	Water Mint	*Mentha aquatica*
6	Purple Loosestrife	*Lythrum salicaria*

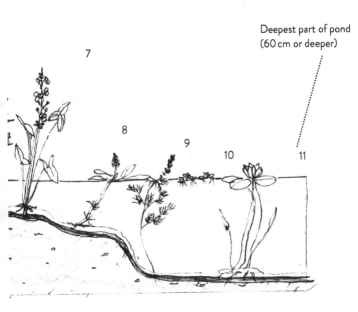

Deepest part of pond
(60 cm or deeper)

7	Arrowhead	*Sagittaria latifolia sagittifolia*
8	Amphibious Bistort	*Persicaria amphibium*
	also known as	*Polygonum amphibium*
9	Spiked Water Milfoil	*Hyriophyllum spicatun*
10	Water Starwort	*Callitriche spp.*
11	White Water Lily	*Nymphaea alba*

Pond Liner

At this point, other than a few pegs in the grass and a bit of sand, you haven't committed to anything. So it's time to consider the item that will be the chief expense: the liner. Some lucky people may be able to use puddled clay to line their new ponds, but for most of us this won't be an option, and a liner will be the solution. Liners are not cheap and you'll need a much bigger one than you initially might think.

A simple rule of thumb for working out the size of the liner you need is as follows. First, measure the maximum length, width and depth of the pond. Then:

- For the length of the liner, take the length of the pond, add twice the depth, and add 50cm.
- For the width of the liner, take the width of the pond, add twice the depth, and add 50cm.

The extra amounts are so that you can anchor the edges of the liner in a small trench around the pond. Don't forget: you'll need to add more liner area if you're considering a bog-garden at one end. You may choose to construct a substantial bog-garden as an overflow system by extending the liner, perforating the bog section with small holes and covering the bog-garden base with small pebbles to prevent soil blocking the holes.

Types of Pond Liner

What sort of liner do you need? If you have a really large area, you might consider using a geo-textile/bentonite product from companies such as Bentomat and Rawell, but they require very gentle, smooth gradients, so they're not really feasible for small ponds. For most of us, there are four possibilities: polythene, PVC, ethylene propylene rubber (EPDM) and butyl rubber. Polythene is much the cheapest but is also the least reliable and probably has the shortest life. Some new forms of PVC/underlay packages from manufacturers such as Blagdon are worth considering. But all the ponds I've so far been involved with have been either lined with EPDM from companies such as Firestone or SealEco Greenseal, or the more expensive but perhaps longer-lasting butyl rubber products from suppliers such as Butyl Products Ltd. Most people opt for EPDM as it represents good value for money.

Opt for a dark-coloured liner: paler ones can reflect heat back into the pond and have been known to promote the growth of blanket weed (see the 'Managing your pond' chapter).

What Lies Beneath

So, you've decided on the type of liner. Now you need to consider what should lie between it and the soil beneath. Nowadays it's possible to purchase purpose-made underlay and if you can afford it, it's probably best. But hundreds of ponds have been protected by less expensive alternatives: old carpet, carpet underlay, thick layers of newspapers and often a combination of all three. Whatever you choose, I'd recommend covering the floor and sides of the pond hole with a 6cm-layer of sand before you do anything. For our demonstration garden pond at the former National Dragonfly Museum, we laid a bed of sand, then newspapers, then a horrible, old, yellow, seriously stained carpet that someone had thrown away.

Before you begin to dig, it's important to decide where you plan to put the spoil and whether you want to separate the topsoil from the layers below. Of course it can all be carted away to fulfil some other purpose in the garden, but many people elect to create a small bank to the north-east of the pond; even a rockery. This gives another dimension to the area and, once again, gives you the chance to add interesting plants and more colour to your garden. It's also a place for dragonflies to bask, sheltered from the north and east winds. And if your dragonflies choose to emerge on plants at the northern and western ends – having moved up the gentle gradients I advised – there will be less chance of the wind bashing the newly-adult dragonflies against other plants and damaging their fragile wings as they expand.

Spoil Removal

If you intend to throw the spoil onto grass before moving it, it's best to lay a big sheet of polythene down to protect the grass. A sheet like that is also useful for hauling smaller quantities of earth around the garden, using the sheet as a sort of sledge.

If you're digging up a lawn, it's worth taking off the turf carefully and setting it aside, as you may wish to lay it round the edges of the pond once you have finished. Decent sized turves will make a very nice border round the bog area, should you choose to create one.

Digging

When it comes to actually digging the pond, there's no advice except 'get stuck in'. It's hard work and it's easy to overdo it, so take it gently and pause for breaks. You might consider digging a test hole first. Some potential pond constructors have done this, found it much harder than they'd imagined and, as a result, decided to hire a small digger. You may want to do the same. Remember to dig deeper than the planned depth of the pond, as you must allow for the depth of the sand and other material beneath the liner.

Before you actually lay the liner, I suggest you dig a shallow trench around the outside so that you can drop the edges of the liner into it and anchor it with stones (though you should not begin anchoring it in place until after you've filled the pond with water). You may also choose to lay paving slabs, and these will give you similar firm anchorage as well as convenient places to watch what takes place on your new pond. It's really up to you. Paving slabs will add a little formality and convenience, whereas stones will give your pond a more 'wild' feel. You might like to have both, so that you have direct access to some parts of the pond edge with slabs, and other parts are 'wilder' with stones.

Whatever you do, don't stretch the liner as you lay it. Let it find its own position and pleat it carefully if necessary.

If you're planning a really very large pond, it would be wise to check with the Environment Agency – or the Scottish Environmental Protection Agency, if you're in Scotland – to be sure you're adhering to legal requirements. The same advice holds for damming streams; in that case it's the National Rivers Authority. More information is available on their respective websites, but there is no substitute for personal contact.

Filling the Pond

Filling the pond is a very satisfying task. Fill gently and slowly. Wait a couple of days after you have filled it before anchoring the liner in place. This gives time for the liner to find its own shape and, if you're using mains water, will allow chlorine to release into the air. Then you can begin the planting.

If you have a pond nearby that is fully established – but free of fish – a few buckets of water from it, together with muddy substrate from the bottom, will accelerate smaller animal life activity. Remember to ask permission if it's not yours.

Don't be too horrified if your pond goes murky or coffee-coloured. This sometimes happens at the start. It tends to be a spring phenomenon. Just be patient and, aided by plant action and tiny life forms, it should clear by itself.

Planting Up the Pond

Choosing the Right Plants to Suit Your Pond

As a general rule, the best time for putting in water plants is late spring and early summer, and I recommend using local native water plants, many of which are colourful little explosions of blues, yellows and reds. This keeps your pond in harmony with the local environment. But for added colour it's possible to use hybrids of local native species and cultivars, such as ornamental lilies in the pond and elegant irises close to the water's edge. See pages 56–59 for recommended plants to use in or near your pond.

The Right Sort of Water

It's important at this stage to know what sort of water you're using: whether it's acidic or alkaline. It's also a good idea, for the same reason, to know what sort of soil you're using as a substrate. This is because certain types of plants prefer acid water and soil, and some prefer alkaline. Of course, many plants are quite happy to thrive in any type of combination. It's easy to obtain a pH test kit from your local garden centre. If your water is above 7pH it's alkaline, and below 7pH it's acidic. Rainwater in the UK is typically slightly acidic.

Some plants thrive in flowing water and others grow best in still water, so if you have a pond only, you'll need to obtain the still-water ones. Check the list below to see what suits your garden.

This quadrant of still/flowing/acid/alkaline applies directly to dragonflies, too. Some like flowing acidic water, some like still alkaline, and so on; and some are quite happy with almost anything, as long as the water quality is good.

Proper Aquatic Baskets

With rubber liners there's always the risk of punctures and so I recommend using proper aquatic baskets placed on the bottom of the pond as a way to avoid this. Many of the plants you choose will benefit from starting in these baskets. Make sure that the ones you buy are of the proper aquatic sort, ones that allow water to pass in.

You can adjust the height of plants with clean bricks laid carefully on the liner. Some suppliers attach little weights to clumps of oxygenating plants, so you can just chuck them in and let them get cracking, but fine gravel – washed beforehand – is also a good way to anchor submerged oxygenating plants. Your pond will acquire a substrate over time, but too much soil to start with can cause outbreaks of blanket weed.

Planting Up the Pond

The Right Compost

In order to avoid chemicals and excess nutrients in your pond, it's important that you use peat-fee aquatic compost, although if you decide to plant non-native aquatic irises you'll find they prefer ordinary garden compost – but make sure it's free of peat, fertilisers and herbicides.

Sourcing Local Native Water Plants

It's quite possible to obtain local native plants from local sources such as farm ponds and friends' ponds. But you *must* obtain permission from the pond owner. It's also important to be sure that what you are taking is both local and native, as many ponds are now over-run by highly invasive non-native species such as, among others, New Zealand Pigmyweed (*Crassula helmsii*) and Water Fern (*Azolla filiculoides*).

Please take great care when buying aquatic plants from garden centres and shops that sell items for aquaria. In some cases they may offer you plants that will do your pond no good at all. Much better to spend a little more money and obtain plants from reputable suppliers such as Hazelwood Landscapes or Wild Flower Shop. The Royal Horticultural Society website (www.rhs.org.uk) has an excellent list of suppliers.

Dragonfly-Friendly Gardening

At our Dragonfly Sanctuary at Ashton Water we obtained plants such as Greater Pondweed (*Potamogeton natans*) from local farm ponds (with permission from the farmers) and purchased others – Flowering Rush (*Butomus umbellatus*), for example – from suppliers.

Be sure to rinse your plants carefully before putting them into your pond.

We've made a list of about 30 attractive water plants likely to suit most ponds, together with suggestions as to the best positions for them. Most of the plants we recommend really like the bright sunshine so essential for dragonfly activity, but one or two are happier in slight shade and we have marked them on the list. We would unhesitatingly recommend all of these plants to pond owners, but be prepared for surprises. Plants don't always obey orders: some may not like your pond at all; others may choose to thrive – and sometimes over-thrive – in unlikely circumstances. A rough guide follows.

In the Water

- **Water Starwort** (*Callitriche stagnalis* or *hermaphroditica*): No special water preferences. Excellent oxygenator and surface coverer. Doesn't mind partial shade. S/W/E

- **Hornwort** (*Ceratophyllum demersum*): No special water preferences. Good oxygenator. Common in south and east of England.

- **Spiked Water Milfoil** (*Myriophyllum spicatum*): No special water preferences. Likes full sun. Good oxygenator. S/W

- **Curled Pondweed** (*Potamogeton crispus*): No special water preferences. Very good oxygenator.

- **Water Crowfoot** (*Ranunculus aquatilis*): No special water preferences. Good oxygenator. White flowers on surface. S/W

- **Frogbit** (*Hydrocharis morsus-ranae*): Prefers alkaline water. Little yellow flowers. Commoner in south and east of England.

In / On the Water

- **Greater Pondweed** (*Potamogeton natans*): No special water preferences. Very good surface coverer.

- **Fringed Water Lily** (*Nymphoides peltata*): No special water preferences. Bright yellow flowers. Very attractive but can be vigorous. Commoner in south and east of England. S/W

- **White Water Lily** (*Nymphaea alba*): No special water preferences. Happy in full sun. Plant in baskets. S/W

- **Yellow Water Lily** (*Nuphar lutea*): Prefers slightly acidic water. Can be invasive. *Nuphar* *pumila* is its smaller cousin.

- **Amphibious Bistort** (*Polygonum amphibium*):
Likes still and slow water. Red flowers. Good
surface coverer.

- **Brooklime** (*Veronica beccabunga*): No special
water preferences. Pink or blue flowers.

- **Water Mint** (*Mentha aquatica*): No special water preferences. Pale mauve flowers. Vigorous.
Plant in baskets.

- **Water Forget-Me-Not** (*Myosotis scorpioides*):
No special water preferences. Blue, pink or
white flowers. S/W/E

Around the Edges

- **Water Plantain** (*Alisma plantago-aquatica*):
Likes slow to still water. Tiny yellow/white/
pink flowers.

- **Flowering Rush** (*Butomus umbellatus*): Likes
to be in rather than beside water. Pink/white
flowers. Tall and attractive. Commoner in south
and east of England. S/W

- **Yellow Flag Iris** (*Iris pseudacorus*): Prefers acid
water. Doesn't mind partial shade. Very vigorous. Plant in baskets or just beyond the edge of
liner. S/E

- **Soft Rush** (*Juncus effusus*): Likes acid water.
Doesn't mind partial shade. Some damselflies
like to lay eggs in floating, dead rush – so don't
tidy it up too much. S/W/E

- **Bog Bean** (*Menyanthes trifoliata*): Prefers acid

water and likes slow to still water. White/pink flowers. Plant in baskets.

- **Marsh Marigold** (*Caltha palustris*): Happy at the edge of almost any water space. Bright yellow flowers. Likes full sun. S/W

- **Branched Bur-reed** (*Sparganium erectum*): No special water preferences. Often used by dragonflies for emergence.

- **Greater Spearwort** (*Ranunculus lingua*): No special water preferences. Yellow flowers. Less common in parts of Scotland and Wales.

- **Lesser Spearwort** (*Ranunculus flammula*): No special water preferences. Yellow flowers. Common across the UK.

- **Marsh Speedwell** (*Veronica scutellata*): No special water preferences. Small white, blue or purplish flowers. Common across the UK.

- **Marsh Bedstraw** (*Galium palustre*): No special water preferences. White flowers. Common across the UK.

- **Arrowhead** (*Sagittaria sagittifolia*): No special water preferences. White flowers with purple centres. Can be invasive. Plant in baskets.

Close to the Pond

There are also plants that are attractive and are happy being close to the water's edge. They're attractive both for being decorative, and by appealing to insects as prey for dragonflies.

These include pale maroon **Hemp Agrimony** (*Eupatorium cannabinum* – no relation, by the way!), bright white-and-yellow **Ox-Eye Daisy** (*Leucanthemum vulgare*) and Purple **Loosestrife** (*Lythrum salicaria*), which likes to be S/E and is scarcer – though perfectly growable – in Scotland. All these are vigorous and may need controlling. It's best if you plant them *beside* rather than *on* the liner.

A selection of **Primula** species and **Snake's-head Fritillary** (*Fritillaria meleagris*) will also provide colour around the edges of your pond.

Links Between Plants and Dragonflies

Surprisingly perhaps, we're not really able to say, 'If you put in Plant A into your pond, you will get Dragonfly B.' This is because, over the years, dragonfly enthusiasts have tended to concentrate on recording where dragonflies live rather than which plants they consistently use. But a recent study has shown that a newly arrived colonist, the Small Red-eyed Damselfly (*Erythromma viridulum*), has a marked preference for sites that have Hornwort (*Ceratophyllum demersum*), which is present in the south and east of England. Several

plants are known to be attractive to specific dragonflies, but there's room for more work on this
subject and we have run many courses to enable
dragonfly enthusiasts to identify water plants.
What we can say with certainty is that the greater
the variety of water plants you put in your pond,
the greater the number of species you will attract.

When we set up Ashton Water Dragonfly
Sanctuary in 1989, we first had to stop Père
David's deer wading into the lake. These
monarch-of-the-glen sized water-loving beasts
had turned the lake into a mudbath, so, with
funding from the WWF, we fenced the lake off.
That year we saw only five species of dragonfly
and damselfly at the lake. By 1994, by virtue of
allowing plants to regenerate, and by putting
in a wide selection of local native water plants,
we had increased the number of dragonflies and
damselflies seen to the seventeen I mentioned
earlier. Not all were breeding in the lake, but we
had made a significant difference nevertheless.

Before I list any connections between particular plants and specific species of dragonfly, I should point out straight away that what is listed below is by no means definitive, and when owners of existing ponds and dragonfly enthusiasts read on, from their own experience they will immediately want to add other dragonflies and plants.

But at least ten water plants have been quite specifically recorded as being used by ten particular species of dragonfly and damselfly, either for perching or emerging or, most importantly, egg-laying.

Here are the ten plants known to be used by dragonflies and damselflies:

- Spiked Water Milfoil

- Hornwort

- Curled Pondweed

- Frogbit

- Sphagnum Moss

- Water Mint

- Soft Rush

- Flowering Rush

- Yellow Flag Iris

- White Water Lily

And here are ten dragonflies and damselflies that use them:

- Common Blue Damselflies: Soft Rush and Curled Pondweed.

- Azure Damselflies: Spiked Water Milfoil, White Water Lily, Frogbit, Curled Pondweed and Hornwort.

- Blue-tailed Damselflies: Spiked Water Milfoil, Water Mint, Frogbit, Soft Rush and Flowering Rush.

- Large Red Damselflies: Curled Pondweed, Hornwort and Water Mint.

- Emerald Damselflies: Soft Rush, Flowering Rush and Yellow Iris.

- Four-spotted Chasers: Curled Pondweed, Spiked Water Milfoil and White Water Lily.

- Common Hawkers: Soft Rush, Yellow Flag Iris and Sphagnum Moss.

- Migrant Hawkers: Soft Rush.

- Southern Hawkers: Yellow Flag Iris.

- Emperors: Spiked Water Milfoil, White Water Lily, Hornwort and Curled Pondweed.

It would be very good to add to these lists and we look forward to being given further specific examples from fellow dragonfly enthusiasts and DFG pond owners.

Dragonfly-Friendly Gardening

Bur-reed

Loosestrife

Yellow Flag Iris

Flowering Rush

White Water Lily

Seeing What Comes

You will be surprised how quickly life materialises in your new pond. There's absolutely no need to import dragonflies, either in egg or larval form. In fact, it's not a good idea, as you may be importing larvae that really aren't suitable for your pond. In any case, if your pond is right – and has the right water plants – they will come of their own accord. It may take some time for dragonflies to begin to breed in your pond, but you'll fairly certainly have visitors almost immediately, especially if you have another dragonfly pond within a radius of about three miles of yours. On one occasion – at Highgrove in Gloucestershire – I was still in the act of putting the first plants in a brand new pond when a Broad-bodied Chaser arrived to check out the new habitat with a view to laying her eggs.

To get a rough idea of the species visiting your pond, have a look at the diagrams on pages 26–29, which show the shapes of typical dragon-flies. Why not photograph your visitors? You'll be able to build up a collection of images showing them hunting, perching, mating and ovipositing (laying eggs). Besides, photographs will enable you to identify the species that have chosen your pond. If you're in the UK, the quickest way to identify your local dragonflies is to check the British Dragonfly Society's website. It has comprehensive and detailed information to help you track dragonfly activity around your pond. There are also extremely good dragonfly books that concentrate almost entirely on identification and these are listed in the 'Further Reading and Resources' section.

I find that a pair of close-focus binoculars really helps me with identification. Having them slung around my neck when I'm beside the water enables me to grab them quickly, and I delight in close-up views of the amazing colours of these insects. The British Dragonfly Society is always keen to know of any dragonfly activity and it's easy to record what you see on their website (www.british-dragonflies.org.uk).

Your first arrivals may well be males, looking to set up their territory. Male dragonflies set up and guard territory, flying up and down, driving away any other males of the same species and waiting for females to arrive. If they see a female, they will immediately attempt to mate. The male has a pair of claspers on the end of his abdomen and he will seize the female round the neck, and together they will form a sort of heart shape. They can fly and mate at the same time. The females are ready to lay eggs immediately. Different species lay eggs in different ways. In the case of many larger dragon-flies and smaller damselflies the females will cut holes in vegetation and insert their eggs, but many medium-sized dragonflies just touch their abdo-mens onto the surface and shoot their eggs into the water to sink down to the bottom of the pond.

In some cases the females fly in tandem with the males, as the males wish to guard the females while they pass on their genes. Two pairs of powerful eyes are better than one, and four pairs of wings can be useful if an emergency getaway is required. If you see any of this activity, you can shout, 'Ovipositing!' because that's exactly what they're doing, and it's very good news for you as it means they're voting for your pond with their offspring.

Don't expect immediate results from the ovi-positing activity, however, as many damselflies can spend about a year under water before they emerge as adults. Dragonflies can take two, sometimes three years, or even longer. In the meantime, you can keep an eye on what is hap-pening below the surface by doing a touch of pond-dipping occasionally. For this you will need a standard-size kitchen sieve (the Scots dragonfly folk prefer colanders, but it's up to you) and a white plastic tray. Be prepared to get dirty knees. Kneel down beside the margin of your pond and guddle the sieve among the underwater plants.

Go in swiftly and firmly against the edge, guddle a quick, easy arm-swing along, and lift out the contents of your sieve into the tray. With luck, among the other creepy-crawlies, you'll find tiny damselfly and dragonfly larvae. Larvae can 'play dead', so have patience. Have a look at the diagrams on pages 29–31 to see what you have found. They're simplified, so if you want to research further there is a list of books for you in the 'Further Reading and Resources' section.

If you have lilies in your pond, why not gently turn the edges over. If it looks as though someone has been doing a little sewing on the underside, you're looking at where a damselfly has laid her eggs.

When it's time for the larvae to emerge, you may well spot one clambering up a plant stem. Put down whatever you're doing and just watch one of the miracles of nature right in front of your eyes. You will see the new adult split the skin of the larval case, haul itself out, slowly expand into its full adult shape, and finally fly away. The amazing little case it leaves behind is called an exuvia and it is the perfect proof of what species you have breeding in your pond. Each species can be identified from its exuvia. There's an excellent British Dragonfly Society guidebook – *Field Guide to the Larvae and Exuviae of British*

Dragonflies, by Steve Cham – to help you to do this, although in some cases you will need a hand lens, and with a few species, even a microscope! Be careful how you handle exuviae: they're fragile, paper-thin, feather-light, and they're often clamped firmly onto their chosen stems. You might consider taking your exuviae collection along to a British Dragonfly Society event. Let them do the identification for you, and learn a bit more at the same time.

Of course, you will also begin to spot other arrivals at your pond: Great Diving Beetles, Stoneflies, Pond Skimmers, Water Boatmen, Pond Skaters, Whirlygig Beetles and so on; also bloodworms and mosquito larvae, both of which are excellent food for dragonfly larvae. I mentioned their amazing mouthparts earlier: dragonfly and damselfly larvae both have an astonishing labial mask mounted under their heads; it can shoot out, like an arm with claws on the end, to grab prey and feed it back into their mouthparts. They're real underwater monsters. Have another look at the illustration on page 29.

A Few Amazing Facts About Dragonflies

- Dragonfly larvae have gills in their abdomens and breathe through their backsides. They can suck water in and blast it out to propel themselves through the water.

- Dragonflies are among the fastest fliers in the insect world. Some are reckoned to fly at nearly 40mph. Horseflies are faster, but only in a straight line.

- Dragonfly agility is aided by a protein molecule called resilin. It's the most elastic protein in the world, and works best in warm conditions. The legendary leap of the flea is powered by resilin.

- Some dragonflies can fly huge distances. Hawkers fly over the English Channel, Darters cross the North Sea and Green Darners have even arrived in Cornwall from North America.

- Dragonflies create their own airflows, giving them five times the lift of a conventional aircraft. Their flight characteristics are being studied by air forces for use in unmanned aerial vehicles.

A Few Amazing Facts About Dragonflies

- Dragonflies have almost 360° vision and 80% of their brain function is for processing visual information.

- Some adults have 30,000 lenses and photoreceptors in each eye and they can see polarised ultra-violet light.

- The vision-receiving proteins – opsins – in the eyes of a dragonfly give them up to (a hard to imagine) 10 times better vision than us.

Managing Your Pond

Just like any other part of the garden, your pond needs to be managed and cared for. This, of course, goes for ponds that have been modified for dragonflies as well as for new ponds. It's very important to keep an eye on how your water plants are performing. Some will thrive and others may lag behind. Very often the plants that thrive will be the ones that try to take over. It's best to control them on a little-and-often basis, if possible. Done like this, you'll find that your pond is easy to look after, and it will be a thrill to see all the various plants come to life before your eyes.

Dragonflies like a definite space of clear water, not totally cluttered with plants, so bear that in mind. Once most plant species are established, if you see that a particular one is dominant, you can consider reducing it by at least half. Autumn is the best time. If it transpires that a particular species of plant is becoming seriously invasive, it may well be worth removing it completely. Often it's marginal plants that are the most vigorous and need to be kept under control, but **Amphibious Bistort** and **Fringed Water Lily** need to be watched carefully.

Some of the plants in the wild that dragonflies like to oviposit into are highly invasive in small ponds and in some cases can puncture liners. We've made a list of the main culprits – see below and the following page – most of which are fine on larger water spaces, but with smaller ponds it's definitely best to avoid them. Remember to leave whatever you take out beside the pond for a couple of days so that the insects attached to the vegetation have time to return to the pond.

Keep your water level up. If you have to resort to mains water, ideally leave it to stand in a bucket for a couple of days before putting it in. This will release chlorine and allow the temperature to equalise. A sudden blast of cold water shot into a pond can upset its equilibrium.

When leaves start to fall in autumn, try to keep as many as possible from dropping into the pond. Too much dying vegetation won't help the quality of your water. However, it's worth bearing in mind that some dragonfly larvae use bottom-sunk leaves as cover, so don't worry about being too meticulous.

Some dragonflies oviposit in mud and moss, some will lay eggs in grass surrounding the pond edge, and some have a penchant for using old wet wood. So a soggy log, half in and half out of the water, may be more useful than it looks.

Blanket Weed

You have sited your pond in a sunny spot and so it's possible that, early on, it may suffer from attacks of blanket weed. This is a general term that covers various sorts of algal bloom, including a pea-soup effect in the water and blue-green algae floating on the surface, but specifically it refers to mats of green filamentous algae choking the water. These attacks are usually as a result of excessive nutrients – from mains water, for example, or agricultural runoff – combined with insufficient oxygenating plants under the water and lack of surface coverers that provide shade beneath the surface. Once a balance has been established, your pond will generally right itself. But you can remove filamentous algae by what we call the 'cocktail stick' method. The best tool is a broom handle, twirled into the algae. Lift the algae out – it's surprisingly heavy – and lay it beside the pond for a couple of days, so that any animal life clinging to it can return to the pond, and then dispose of it. If you leave it on stone or slabs it will dry faster and speed up the process.

In order to avoid build-up of blanket weed, many pond owners now float small mesh bags of barley straw (sometimes with added lavender) during the spring, and remove them in late autumn. In most cases it seems to be effective, and it appears to work best if water is passed through it, which is fine if you have a stream, but otherwise it might be worth placing the barley straw at the point where your rainwater feeds into the pond.

Three Other Nasties

Three other unpleasant invaders that we have experienced are **Duckweed** (*Lemna* species), **New Zealand Pigmyweed** (*Crassula helmsii*) and **Water Fern** (*Azolla filiculoides*). If left alone, these can rapidly cover the surface of a pond, blacking out any life beneath. In all three cases we used sieves, and sieves on poles, to scoop it out. If you have to do it, put the stuff on the compost heap. Keep a watchful eye and don't let any of them reappear.

Plants Only Suitable for Really Big Waterspaces

- **Great Reed Mace** (*Typha latifolia*): This is extremely invasive and if seen in a small pond it's worth removing immediately. It is often the start of recolonisation of disused ponds by larger bushes and crack willows. Its slimmer cousin, Lesser Reed Mace (*Typha angustifolia*), is more acceptable.

- **Reed** (*Phragmites australis*): Once this plant is established it needs constant management. Dragonflies really like it, as do thatchers, but it's too big for smaller ponds.

- **Sweet grasses** (*Glyceria* species): Very invasive and dense.

- **Sedge** (*Carex* species): Invasive and sharp-edged.

Enjoying Your Garden

You've done all the hard work and now it's time to sit back, relax and enjoy your creation. You've added another dimension to your garden and brought new interest, colour and life. You'll get to know the species of dragonfly and damselfly that have decided your pond is a fine place to be. You can feel really good that you have reduced the deficit of dragonfly homes just a little, and tipped the balance of your garden a bit more in nature's favour. You'll surprise yourself at the delight you'll feel when you see your first dragonfly emerge from beneath the water surface, climb up a stem you yourself have planted, haul itself slowly out of its larval skin and turn into a beautiful flying creature right in front of you.

I never cease to be amazed and delighted by the number of people who proudly tell me the exact number of a particular species that has emerged from their pond in a summer, a species that, by the way, they can now identify with scarcely more than a glance. You'll find yourself wondering which other visitors have arrived. Besides all the beetles and bugs, there will be frogs or toads, maybe newts too.

Take a sunny summer afternoon, settle back in a chair for a good half-hour or more, maybe with a glass of something refreshing, and just watch. This is the very best bit. In a sense you're back to just watching, in the same way as you did when you spent a little time at your favourite bankside spot, only now that spot is here in your garden and you'll probably have a chair to sit in this time.

Just watch. Take your time. You're a DFG. It's part of the job. You will be amazed at how much you'll see – and learn – from just relaxing by the water's edge. It's good for you, and it's good for dragonflies.

I was having a cup of tea with a friend in her kitchen recently when a neighbour dropped in for a chat. Perhaps unsurprisingly the conversation turned to dragonflies, and the neighbour began to smile. She had, she said, just come back from a very tough spell nursing someone with severe dementia, the sort that wakes the house into action at least five times a night. At one point, just when she thought she was going to crack, a relative arrived and enabled her to get a brief break. For the first time in many days and nights she went out into the sunny late-morning garden, sat down by the pond and began to relax. And, she said, it was the sight of the dragonflies and damselflies – little shards of colour, silently speeding about their business – that restored her and raised her spirits again.

In Buddhism, dragonflies represent 'awareness of self'. In China, they're symbols of prosperity, harmony and good luck. In Japan, at the Bon Festival on the 15th of August, a particular species – the Wandering Glider (*Pantala flavescens*) – is believed to carry ancestral souls home. Japanese emperors wrote poems about them, and Samurai used dragonflies as symbols of power, agility and victory.

Native Americans traditionally revered drag-onflies, and the Navajo would mark rocks beside ponds with a dragonfly cross to indicate the purity of the water. And, as you now know, they were quite right.

In Christianity, the way that a dragonfly larva changes from its underwater larval existence into a wonderful flying insect – a new life about which it cannot know until it makes the change – is sometimes used to help grieving children understand about the possibility of an afterlife.

In the seventeenth century, the Dutch painters who produced those gorgeous flower paintings included insects in their work. Each insect was a symbol, and for them, dragonflies represented 'the resurrection of the contemplative soul'.

So my newfound nursing friend is not alone in finding her spirits lifted. It's a feeling I personally know very well. Ever since that first dragonfly landed on my shirt all those years ago, the feeling hasn't changed; each time I see a dragonfly zooming past I get a cheerful little spiritual nudge, and my heart lifts. Is it to do with their beauty and agility? Is it to do with the fact that versions of these delightful fierce creatures have been around for not far short of 350 million years, and, compared to them, our human race has been here for scarcely a tick of the Earth's clock? What is it? I really don't know. It's a mystery. Perhaps you understand already, but if not, I've got a feeling you will, fairly shortly. As Albert Einstein said, 'The most beautiful thing we can experience is the mysterious. It is the source of all true art and science.'

So, if you have a pond, get cracking on making it attractive for dragonflies. And, if you haven't, get digging! Every pond counts!

Further Reading and Resources

British Dragonfly Society

www.british-dragonflies.org.uk, a charity established in 1983. As their excellent website states, the society is "the voice for dragonflies in Britain" and its key aims are to "improve understanding and awareness of dragonflies, their conservation and the challenges they face, in order to increase action for dragonflies across Britain." The society welcomes questions and comments and is a source of friendly and helpful advice, support and encouragement.

Dragonfly Books

- Steve Brooks and Richard Lewington, *Field Guide to the Dragonflies and Damselflies of Great Britain and Ireland*, British Wildlife Publishing, 1997. This is the book I turn to first.

- Dave Smallshire and Andy Swash, *Britain's Dragonflies: A Field Guide to the Damselflies and Dragonflies of Britain and Ireland*, 3rd edition, Princeton University Press, 2014. Another excellent field guide. This book is also available as an app, really very useful, especially if you have your phone or tablet by the pond.

- Klaas-Douwe B Dijkstra, *Field Guide to the Dragonflies of Britain and Europe*, British Wildlife Publishing, 2020.

Dragonfly-Friendly Gardening

- David Chandler and Steve Cham, *Dragonfly*, New Holland Publishers, 2013. A straightforward, easy to read text, with some wonderful photos.

- Ruary Mackenzie Dodds, *The Dragonfly Diaries*, Saraband, 2014. Inspirational adventure!

- Steve Cham, *Field Guide to the Larvae and Exuviae of British Dragonflies*, British Dragonfly Society, 2012. Superbly thorough, this a very useful tool for identifying which particular species are breeding in your pond. Careful collection and identification of exuviae attached to the vegetation in and around your pond is a fascinating and useful study in its own right.

Other Dragonfly Books, Out of Print but Worth Hunting Down for the Really Keen:

- Philip Corbet, Cynthia Longfield and Norman Moore, *Dragonflies*, Collins New Naturalist, 1960. The first comprehensive summary.

- Bob Gibbons, *Dragonflies and Damselflies of Great Britain and Europe*, Hamlyn, 1994. Includes some good photos, useful for identification.

- Cyril Hammond, *The Dragonflies of Great Britain and Ireland*, Harley Books, 1985. Lovely illustrations.

- Philip Corbet, *Dragonflies: Behaviour and Ecology of Odonata*, Harley Books, 1999. The bible for dragonflies. And his earlier book: *A Biology of Dragonflies*, Quadrangle Books, 1963.

- Georg and Dagmar Rüppell, *Jewelwings*, Georg Rüppell, 2006. Superb photographs.

- Colin Twist and Dan Powell, *A Guide to the Dragonflies of Great Britain*, Arlequin Publications, 1999.

- Peter Miller, *Dragonflies*, 2nd revised edition, Richmond Publishing, 1995. A good book to use for student projects.

- Andy McGeeney, *A Complete Guide to British Dragonflies*, Jonathan Cape, 1986.

- Jill Silsby, *Dragonflies of the World*, CSIRO Publishing, 2001.

Other Dragonfly Resources

The British Dragonfly Society. An excellent resource for all things dragonfly, the society's website (www.british-dragonflies.org.uk) also sells many of the above books. The BDS has 1,500 lively members, a splendid Annual Indoor Meeting, a terrific magazine, and is well worth joining. The BDS runs a DragonflyWatch programme, where members of the public are encouraged to submit their records about dragonfly sightings. Collating this important information will help build knowledge and steer conservation priorities. Every June, the BDs runs an annual Pondwatch event on Twitter/X, which swaps garden stories and videos from across Britain. Professional film-makers such as Steve

White and Will Clothier share their work, and advice is available from Ruary's fellow Dragonfly Ambassadors, Joel Ashton and Green-fingered George. You can follow them at @_joelashton and @GreenFGeorge. Check the BDS website for more details.

The two main international dragonfly organisations are:

- Worldwide Dragonfly Association (worlddragonfly.org)

- *Societas Internationalis Odonatologica* (www.odonatologica.com)

Pond Books

- Alan Titchmarsh, *Water Gardening*, BBC Books, 2013. An excellent, practical, understandable guide.

- Richard Orton and Anne and John Bebbington, *Guide to Commoner Water Plants*, Field Studies Council, 2000. Although this is not strictly a book, more a leaflet, it's a very useful, highly detailed – and virtually waterproof – guide to aquatic plants.

- Richard Orton and Anne and John Bebbington, *The Freshwater Name Trail: A Key to Invertebrates of Ponds and Streams*, Field Studies Council, 1998. This is great for working out what other sorts of beasts you have in your pond. It's in the same format as the one above.

- Greg and Sue Speichert, *Encyclopedia of Water Garden Plants*, Timber Press, 2004.

- John Stephen Hicks, *The Pond Book,* Fitzhenry and Whiteside, 2013.

Other Pond Books that are Out of Print but Worth Trying to Dig Up:

- Christopher D Preston and Jane M Croft, *Aquatic Plants in Britain and Ireland*, New edition, Harley Books, 2001. Very thorough.

- Gerald Thompson, Jennifer Coldrey and George Bernard,

- *The Pond*, Collins, 1985.

- Philip Swindells, *Water Gardening*, 1st edition, Penguin, 1985.

- David Spencer-Jones and Max Wade, *Aquatic Plants*, Borcombe, 1986. Good photographs.

Other Pond Resources

The Royal Horticultural Society has an excellent website (www.rhs.org.uk) full of information and advice, well worth consulting.

Binoculars

An indispensable tool for spotting adult dragon-flies is a pair of close-focussing binoculars. Kari uses Pentax 'Papilio' 8.5x21. Ruary uses Pentax 'Papilio' 6.5x21 and finds them perfectly good for longer-range stuff too.

Where to See Dragonflies in the UK

This section provides a list of sites in the UK in which a significant amount of dragonfly species have been recorded. Some are officially designated 'Hotspots', selected by the British Dragonfly Society (BDS) for their variety of species, as well as the opportunities they offer for learning about dragonflies and volunteering in conservation.

For a full list of excellent sites for dragonfly observation in the UK, visit british-dragonflies.org.uk

YORKSHIRE AND HUMBER

Rodley Nature Reserve, West Yorkshire (BDS Designated Hotspot)

Species: Emerald Damselfly, Migrant Hawker, Banded Demoiselle, Southern Hawker, Common Hawker, Brown Hawker, Emperor Dragonfly, Ruddy Darter, Four-spotted Chaser, Broad-bodied Chaser, Black-tailed Skimmer, Common Darter, Azure Damselfly, Large Red Damselfly, Common Blue Damselfly, Blue-tailed Damselfly

Dragonfly-Friendly Gardening

The Yorkshire Arboretum, North Yorkshire
Species: Large Red Damselfly, Migrant Hawker, Ruddy Darter, Southern Hawker, Black-tailed Skimmer, Emperor Dragonfly

WT Coatham Marsh, North Yorkshire
Species: Broad-bodied Chaser, Azure Damselfly, Large Red Damselfly, Black-tailed Skimmer, Common Darter, Common Blue Damselfly

Filey Dams Nature Reserve, North Yorkshire
Species: Black-tailed Skimmer, Broad-bodied Chaser, Common Darter, Brown Hawker, Emperor Dragonfly, Four-spotted Chaser, Ruddy Darter, Southern Hawker, Banded Demoiselle, Black Darter

Oak Road Playing Fields, East Riding Yorkshire
Species: Black-tailed Skimmer, Blue-tailed Damselfly, Brown Hawker, Common Blue Damselfly, Common Darter, Emerald Damselfly, Emperor Dragonfly, Four-spotted Chaser, Migrant Hawker, Ruddy Darter, Small Red-eyed Damselfly

NORTH-EAST ENGLAND

WWT Washington Wetland Centre, Tyne and Wear
Species: Emerald Damselfly, Ruddy Darter, Blue-tailed Damselfly, Azure Damselfly, Common Blue Damselfly, Southern Hawker

Where to See Dragonflies

Falstone Moss, Northumberland

Species: Common Hawker, Emerald Damselfly, Large Red Damselfly, Azure Damselfly, Black Darter, Common Blue Damselfly, Common Darter

NORTH-WEST ENGLAND

WT Summerseat Nature Reserve, Lancashire

Species: Emerald Damselfly, Broad-bodied Chaser, Common Hawker, Southern Hawker, Large Red Damselfly, Azure Damselfly, Common Darter, Brown Hawker

Foulshaw Moss, Cumbria

Species: Four-spotted Chaser, Common Darter, Black Darter, White-faced Darter, Brown Hawker, Broad-bodied Chaser

Brockholes Nature Reserve, Lancashire

Species: Blue-tailed Damselfly, Broad-bodied Chaser, Brown Hawker, Common Blue Damselfly, Common Darter, Emerald Damselfly, Emperor Dragonfly, Four-spotted Chaser, Large Red Damselfly, Migrant Hawker, Southern Hawker, Azure Damselfly, Banded Demoiselle, Black Darter, Black-tailed Skimmer

South Solways Mosses, Cumbria

Species: Blue-tailed Damselfly, Common Hawker, Southern Hawker, Emperor Dragonfly, Four-spotted Chaser, Common Darter, Black Darter, Migrant Hawker, Banded Demoiselle, Emerald Damselfly, Large Red Damselfly, Azure Damselfly, Common Blue Damselfly

WT Black Lake, Cheshire

Emerald Damselfly, Emperor Dragonfly, Four-spotted Chaser, Hairy Dragonfly, Large Red Damselfly, Migrant Hawker, Ruddy Darter, Southern Hawker, Azure Damselfly, Black Darter, Blue-tailed Damselfly, Broad-bodied Chaser, Brown Hawker, Common Blue Damselfly, Common Darter, Common Hawker

WEST MIDLANDS

Swift Valley Nature Reserve, West Midlands

Species: Banded Demoiselle, Black-tailed Skimmer, Blue-tailed Damselfly, Common Blue Damselfly, Brown Hawker, Common darter, Emperor Dragonfly, Four-Spotted Chaser, Large Red Damselfly, Migrant Hawker, Red-eyed Damselfly, Ruddy Darter, Small Red-eyed damselfly, Southern Hawker, Azure Damselfly

Bateswood, Staffordshire

Species: Broad-bodied Chaser, Brown Hawker, Common Blue Damselfly, Common Darter, Common Hawker, Emerald Damselfly, Emperor Dragonfly, Four-spotted Chaser, Large Red Damselfly, Ruddy Darter, Southern Hawker, Migrant Hawker, Azure Damselfly, Black Darter, Black-tailed Skimmer, Blue-tailed Damselfly

Shropshire Hills Discovery Centre, Shropshire (BDS Designated Hotspot)

Species: Beautiful Demoiselle, Large Red Damselfly, Ruddy Darter, Southern Hawker, White-legged Damselfly, Common Darter, Common Blue Damselfly, Azure Damselfly, Blue-tailed Damselfly, Broad-bodied Chaser, Four-spotted Chaser, Emperor Dragonfly, Brown Hawker, Banded Demoiselle

Venus Pool Nature Reserve, Shropshire

Species: Brown Hawker, Common Blue Damselfly, Common Darter, Emperor Dragonfly, Four-spotted Chaser, Migrant Hawker, Ruddy Darter, Azure Damselfly, Banded Demoiselle, Black-tailed Skimmer, Blue-tailed Damselfly

Willington Wetlands, Derbyshire

Species: Variable Damselfly, Red-eyed Damselfly,

Hairy Dragonfly, Scarce Chaser, Common Darter, Migrant Hawker, Four-spotted Chaser, Blue-tailed Damselfly, Common Blue Damselfly, Azure Damselfly, Banded Demoiselle, Brown Hawker, Broad-bodied Chaser, Black-tailed Skimmer, Emerald Damselfly

EAST MIDLANDS
Attenborough, East Midlands

Ruddy Darter, Southern Hawker, Azure Damselfly, Hairy Dragonfly, Red-eyed Damselfly, Small Red-eyed Damselfly, Banded Demoiselle, Black-tailed Skimmer, Blue-tailed Damselfly, Broad-bodied Chaser, Brown Hawker, Common Blue Damselfly, Common Darter, Emerald Damselfly, Emperor Dragonfly, Four-spotted Chaser, Large Red Damselfly, Migrant Hawker

Baston Fen, Lincolnshire

Species: Common Blue Damselfly, Common Darter, Emerald Damselfly, Emperor Damselfly, Emperor Dragonfly, Four-spotted Chaser, Hairy Dragonfly, Large Red Damselfly, Migrant Hawker, Red-eyed Damselfly, Ruddy Darter, Southern Hawker, Variable Damselfly, Willow Emerald Damselfly, Broad-bodied Chaser, Black-tailed Skimmer, Azure Damselfly, Banded Demoiselle, Blue-tailed Damselfly, Brown Hawker

Where to See Dragonflies

Whisby Nature Reserve Dragonfly, Lincolnshire (BDS Designated Hotspot)

Species: Blue-tailed Damselfly, Black-tailed Skimmer, Common Blue Damselfly, Common Darter, Emerald Damselfly, Emperor Dragonfly, Four-spotted Chaser, Hairy Dragonfly, Large Red Damselfly, Migrant Hawker, Red-eyed Damselfly, Ruddy Darter, Southern Hawker, Willow Emerald Damselfly, Azure Damselfly, Banded Demoiselle, Broad-bodied Chaser, Brown Hawker

Gibraltar Point National Nature Reserve

Species: Emerald Damselfly, Emperor Dragonfly, Four-spotted Chaser, Large Red Damselfly, Migrant Hawker, Ruddy Darter, Small Red-eyed Damselfly, Southern Hawker, Azure Damselfly, Black Darter, Black-Tailed Chaser, Blue-tailed Damselfly, Broad-bodied Chaser, Brown Hawker, Common Blue Damselfly, Common Darter

Saltfleetby–Theddlethorpe Dunes, Lincolnshire

Species: Azure Damselfly, Blue-tailed Damselfly, Broad-Bodied Chaser, Common Blue Damselfly, Common Darter, Emerald Damselfly, Emperor Dragonfly, Four-spotted Chaser, Hairy Dragonfly, Large Red Damselfly, Migrant Hawker, Ruddy Darter, Small Red-eyed Damselfly, Southern Hawker

SOUTH-WEST ENGLAND

Stover country Park, Devon (BDS Designated Hotspot)

Species: Hairy Dragonfly, Keeled Skimmer, Migrant Hawker, Ruddy Darter, Southern Hawker, Azure Damselfly, Common Blue Damselfly, Blue-tailed Damselfly, Emerald Damselfly, Beautiful Demoiselle, Large Red Damselfly, Red-eyed Damselfly, Small Red-eyed Damselfly

WWT Steart Marshes, Somerset (BDS Designated Hotspot)

Species: Emerald Damselfly, Red-eyed Damselfly, Small Red-eyed Damselfly, Brown Hawker, Scarce Chaser, Ruddy Darter, Banded Demoiselle, Beautiful Demoiselle, Southern Hawker, Broad-bodied Chaser

Town Common, Dorset

Species: Black-tailed Skimmer, Blue-tailed Damselfly, Broad-bodied Chaser, Brown Hawker, Common Blue Damselfly, Common Darter, Common Hawker, Downy Emerald

WWT Smallbrook Meadows, Wiltshire

Species: Common Blue Damselfly, Broad-bodied Chaser, Beautiful Demoiselle, Large Red Damselfly,

Common Darter, Banded Demoiselle, Azure
Damselfly, Southern Hawker, Migrant Hawker,
Ruddy Darter, Emperor Dragonfly, Blue-tailed
Damselfly

Cadover Bridge, Devon

Species: Golden-ringed Dragonfly, Keeled Skimmer,
Common Darter, Black Darter, Broad-bodied
chaser, Common Hawker, Emerald Damselfly,
Four-spotted Chaser, Scarce Blue-tailed Damselfly,
Beautiful Demoiselle, Azure Damselfly, Common
Blue Damselfly, Blue-tailed Damselfly, Large Red
Damselfly, Southern Hawker, Emperor Dragonfly

EAST OF ENGLAND

Paxton Pits, Cambridgeshire (BDS Designated Hotspot)

Species: Emerald Damselfly, Emperor Dragonfly,
Four-spotted Chaser, Hairy Dragonfly, Large Red
Damselfly, Migrant Hawker, Norfolk Hawker,
Red-eyed Damselfly, Ruddy Darter, Scarce Chaser,
Southern Hawker, Variable Damselfly, Willow
Emerald Damselfly, Small Red-eyed Damselfly,
White-legged Damselfly, Azure Damselfly, Banded
Demoiselle, Black-tailed Skimmer, Blue-tailed
Damselfly, Brown Hawker, Broad-bodied Chaser,
Common Blue Damselfly, Common Darter

NT Wicken Fen Nature Reserve, Cambridgeshire (BDS Designated Hotspot)

Species:Banded Demoiselle, Broad-bodied Chaser, Four-spotted Damselfly, Large Red Damselfly, Migrant Hawker, Red-eyed Damselfly, Small Red-eyed Damselfly, Variable Damselfly, Hairy Dragonfly, Scarce Chaser, Blue-tailed Damselfly, Common Blue Damselfly, Emperor Dragonfly, Emerald Damselfly, Common Darter, Ruddy Darter, Black-tailed Skimmer, Brown Hawker, Southern Hawker, Azure Damselfly, Willow Emerald Damselfly

Panshanger Park, Hertfordshire (BDS Designated Hotspot)

Species: Common Blue Damselfly, Blue-tailed Damselfly, Large Red Damselfly, Banded Demoiselle, Hairy Dragonfly, Four-spotted Chaser

Lackford Lakes Nature Reserve, Suffolk

Species: Emerald Damselfly, Emperor Dragonfly, Four-spotted Chaser, Hairy Dragonfly, Large Red Damselfly, Migrant Hawker, Red-eyed Damselfly, Ruddy Darter, Small Red-eyed Damselfly, Southern Hawker, Willow Emerald Damselfly, Azure Damselfly, Banded Demoiselle, Black-tailed Skimmer, Blue-tailed Damselfly, Broad-bodied Chaser, Brown Hawker, Common Blue Damselfly, Common Darter

SOUTH-EAST ENGLAND

WWT London Wetland Centre, London (BDS Designated Hotspot)

Species: Hairy Dragonfly, Norfolk Hawker, Small Red-Eyed Damselfly, Scarce Chaser, Willow Emerald Damselfly

Exbury Gardens, Hampshire (BDS Designated Dragonfly Hotspot)

Species: Red-eyed Damselfly, Large Red Damselfly, Black-Tailed Skimmer, Common Darter, Downy Emerald, Emperor Dragonfly, Golden-ringed Dragonfly, Ruddy Darter, Southern Hawker, Small Red-eyed Damselfly, Hairy Dragonfly, Migrant Hawker, Keeled Skimmer, Small Red Damselfly, Azure Damselfly, Beautiful Demoiselle, Blue-tailed Damselfly, Common Blue Damselfly

Wat Tyler Country Park, Essex

Species: Migrant Hawker, Common Darter, Brilliant Emerald, Common Blue Damselfly, Blue-tailed Damselfly, Black-tailed Skimmer, Brown Hawker, Ruddy Darter, Southern Migrant Hawker, Scarce Emerald Damselfly, Red-eyed Damselfly, Hairy Dragonfly, Variable Damselfly

Dragonfly-Friendly Gardening

AT Amberley Wildbrooks Nature Reserve, Sussex

Species: Azure Damselfly, Banded Demoiselle, Blue-tailed Damselfly, Broad-bodied Chaser, Brown Hawker, Common Blue Damselfly, Common Darter, Emerald Damselfly, Emperor Dragonfly, Four-spotted Chaser, Hairy Dragonfly, Large Red Damselfly, Migrant Hawker, Ruddy Darter, Scarce Chaser, Southern Hawker, Variable Damselfly

Thursley Common, Surrey (BDS Designated Hotspot)

Species: Keeled Skimmer, Large Red Damselfly, Red-eyed Damselfly, Ruddy Darter, Small Red Damselfly, Southern Hawker, White-legged Damselfly, Azure Damselfly, Banded Demoiselle, Beautiful Demoiselle, Black Darter, Black-tailed Skimmer, Blue-tailed Damselfly, Brilliant Emerald, Broad-bodied Chaser, Brown Hawker, Common Blue Damselfly, Common Darter, Downy Emerald, Emerald Damselfly, Emperor Dragonfly, Four-spotted Chaser, Golden-ringed Dragonfly

WALES

Llangorse Lake, Powys (BDS Designated Hotspot)

Species: Red-eyed Damselfly, Ruddy Darter, Scarce Blue-tailed Damsefly, Scarce Chaser, Southern Hawker, Variable Damselfly, Azure Damselfly, Banded Demoiselle, Beautiful Demoiselle, Black-tailed Skimmer, Blue-tailed Damselfly, Broad-bodied Chaser, Brown Hawker, Common Blue Damselfly, Common Darter, Emerald Damselfly, Emperor Dragonfly, Four-spotted Chaser, Golden-ringed Dragonfly, Hairy Dragonfly, Large Red Damselfly, Migrant Hawker

RSPB Conwy Nature Reserve, Conwy (BDS Designated Hotspot)

Species: Emerald Damselfly, Large Red Damselfly, Blue-tailed Damselfly, Common Blue Damselfly, Azure Damselfly, Common Hawker, Southern Hawker, Migrant Hawker, Emperor Dragonfly, Broad-bodied Chaser, Four-spotted Chaser, Common Darter

Newport Wetlands and Magor Marsh, Monmouthshire (BDS Designated Hotspot)

Species: Keeled Skimmer, Large Red Damselfly, Migrant Hawker, Ruddy Darter, Azure Damselfly,

Blue-tailed Damselfly, Broad-bodied Chaser, Common Blue Damselfly, Common Darter, Emperor Dragonfly, Four-spotted Chaser, Hairy Dragonfly

WT Cors Ian, County Borough

Species: Common Hawker, Migrant Hawker, Southern Hawker, Keeled Skimmer, Four-spotted Chaser, Emperor Dragonfly, Common Blue Damselfly, Blue-tailed Damselfly, Azure Damselfly, Emerald Damselfly, Large Red Damselfly

RSPB Valley Wetlands, Anglesey

Species: Banded Demoiselle, Emperor Dragonfly, Golden-ringed Dragonfly, Blue-tailed Damselfly, Large Red Damselfly, Common Blue Damselfly, Common Darter, Azure Damselfly, Variable Damselfly, Hairy Dragonfly, Emerald Damselfly, Four-spotted Chaser, Migrant Hawker, Broad-bodied Chaser, Black-tailed Skimmer

SCOTLAND
Caerlaverock Wetland Centre, Dumfriesshire (BDS Designated Hotspot)

Species: Emperor Dragonfly, Common Hawker, Four-spotted Chaser, Common Darter, Black Darter, Emerald Damselfly, Large Red Damselfly, Blue-tailed Damselfly, Common Blue Damselfly, Azure Damselfly

Where to See Dragonflies

Crombie Country Park, Angus (BDS Designated Hotspot)

Species: Black Darter, Common Darter, Common Hawker, Four-spotted Chaser, Large Red Damselfly, Azure Damselfly, Blue-tailed Damselfly, Common Blue Damselfly, Emerald Damselfly

Devilla Forest, Inverness-shire (BDS Designated Hotspot)

Species: Large Red Damselfly, Emerald Damselfly, Blue-tailed Damselfly, Four-spotted Chaser, Southern Hawker, Azure Damselfly, Black Darter, Common Darter, Common Darter, Common Hawker, Common Blue Damselfly

Flanders Moss National Nature Reserve, Stirlingshire (BDS Designated Hotspot)

Species: Common Hawker, Northern Emerald, Common Darter, Black Darter, Four-spotted Chaser, Golden-ringed Dragonfly, Common Blue Damselfly, Large Red Damselfly, Emerald Damselfly, Blue-tailed Damselfly

Gartcosh Local Nature Reserve, Lanarkshire (BDS Designated Hotspot)

Species: Common Blue Damselfly, Azure Damselfly, Blue-tailed Damselfly, Emerald Damselfly, Four-spotted Chaser, Common Darter, Black Darter, Common Hawker, Large Red Damselfly

Greenhead Moss Community Nature Park, Lanarkshire (BDS Designated Hotspot)

Species: Common Darter, Common Hawker, Four-spotted Chaser, Large Red Damselfly, Emerald Damselfly, Azure Damselfly, Black Darter, Blue-tailed Damselfly, Common Blue Damselfly

Morton Lochs, Tentsmuir National Nature Reserve, Fife (BDS Designated Hotspot)

Species: Blue-tailed Damselfly, Common Darter, Emperor Dragonfly, Red-veined Darter, Black Darter, Common Hawker, Four-spotted Chaser, Golden-ringed Dragonfly, Large Red Damselfly, Common Blue Damselfly, Azure Damselfly, Emerald Damselfly

Portmoak Moss, Perthshire (BDS Designated Hotspot)

Species: Black Darter, Common Darter, Four-spotted Chaser, Large Red Damselfly, Common Blue Damselfly, Azure Damselfly, Blue-tailed Damselfly, Emerald Damselfly, Common Hawker

Scotstown Moor Local Nature Reserve, Aberdeenshire (BDS Designated Hotspot)

Species: Common Darter, Common Hawker, Four-spotted Chaser, Large Red Damselfly, Common Blue Damselfly, Azure Damselfly, Emerald Damselfly, Blue-tailed Damselfly

Argaty Red Kites, Perthshire (BDS Designated Hotspot)

Species: Emerald Damselfly, Common Blue Damselfly, Azure Damselfly, Blue-tailed Damselfly, Four-spotted Chaser, Large Red Damselfly, Black Darter, Common Darter, Common Hawker

Where to See Dragonflies in the USA

The sites here are based on recordings of species on iNaturalist. In any of these places, head to a body of standing water to have the best chance of seeing dragonflies.

Limestone Park, Alabaster, Alabama

Species: Halloween Pennant, Eastern Pondhawk, Calico Pennant, Four-spotted Pennant, Blue Dasher, Carolina Saddlebags, Fragile Forktail, Wandering Glider, Red Saddlebags, Two-striped Forceptail

Westchester Lagoon Overlook, Anchorage, Alaska

Species: Lake Darner, Black Meadowhawk, Four-spotted Skimmer, Variable Darner, Sedge Darner, Taiga Bluet, Zigzag Darner, Northern Bluet, Boreal Whiteface

Silverbell Lake, Arizona

Species: Blue Dasher, Mexican Amberwing, Rambur's Forktail, Familiar Bluet, Flame Skimmer, Roseate Skimmer, Variegated Meadowhawk, Blue-ringed Dancer, Red-tailed Pennant, Western Pondhawk, Desert Firetail, American Rubyspot, Black Saddlebags, Common Green Darner, Red Saddlebags

Where to See Dragonflies

War Memorial Park, Little Rock, Arkansas

Species: Eastern Pondhawk, Fragile Forktail,
Blue Dasher, Variable Dancer, Swift Setwing,
Stream Bluet, Eastern Amberwing, Orange Bluet,
Powdered Dancer, Familiar Bluet

Lake Los Carneros, Goleta, Santa Barbara County, California

Species: Flame Skimmer, Blue Dasher, Blue-eyed
Darner, Variegated Meadowhawk, Red Saddlebags,
Tule Bluet, Cardinal Meadowhawk, Vivid Dancer,
Pacific Forktail, Common Green Darner

Denver Botanic Gardens, Denver, Colorado

Species: Great Spreadwing, Plains Forktail, Blue
Dasher, Twelve-spotted Skimmer, Vivid Dancer,
Arroyo Bluet, Familiar Bluet, Common Green
Darner, Paddle-tailer Darner, Striped Meadowhawk

East Rock Park, New Haven, Connecticut

Species: Blue Dasher, Eastern Pondhawk, Variable
Dancer, Eastern Amberwing, Stream Bluet,
Common Whitetail, Fragile Forktail, Great Blue
Skimmer, Halloween Pennant, Slaty Skimmer

Redden State Forest, Georgetown, Delaware

Species: Fragile Forktail, Blue Dasher, Eastern
Pondhawk, Autumn Meadowhawk, Slaty Skimmer,

Banded Pennant, Widow Skimmer, Blue Corporal, Carolina Saddlebags, Common Whitetail

Rainbow Springs State Park, Marion County, Florida

Species: Variable Dancer, Blue Ringed Dancer, Eastern Pondhawk, Slaty Skimmer, Cypress Clubtail, Carolina Saddlebags, Great Blue Skimmer, Common Green Darner, Black-shouldered Spinyleg, Dragonhunter

Ocmulgee Mounds National Historical Park, Macon, Georgia

Species: Eastern Pondhawk, Great Blue Skimmer, Common Whitetail, Blue Dasher, Eastern Amberwing, Ebony Jewelwing, Blue-tipped Dancer, Blackwater Clubtail, Black Saddlebags, Slaty Skimmer

Kathryn Albertson Park, Boise, Idaho

Species: Band-winged Meadowhawk, Twelve-Spotted Skimmer, Western Pondhawk, Eight-spotted Skimmer, Blue Dasher, Paddle-tailed Darner, Dot-tailed Whiteface, Common Whitetail, Spotted Spreadwing, Striped Meadowhawk

Where to See Dragonflies

University of Illinois Arboretum, Champaign, Illinois

Species: Autumn Meadowhawk, Eastern Forktail, Fragile Forktail, Skimming Bluet, Blue Dasher, Eastern Pondhawk, Carolina Saddlebags, Double-striped Bluet, Widow Skimmer, Halloween Pennant

Patoka River National Wildlife Refuge, Indiana

Species: Eastern Pondhawk, Common Whitetail, Blue Dasher, Common Green Darner, Widow Skimmer, Halloween Pennant, Eastern Amberwing, Twelve-spotted Skimmer, Blue-tipped Dancer, Orange Bluet

Prairie Park Nature Centre, Lawrence, Kansas

Species: Widow Skimmer, Eastern Pondhawk, Ebony Jewelwing, Fragile Forktail, Spangled Skimmer, Blue Dasher, Twelve-spotted Skimmer, Common Whitetail, Great Spreadwing, Slaty Skimmer

University Lake, Baton Rouge, Louisiana

Species: Eastern Pondhawk, Blue Dasher, Fragile Forktail, Rambur's Forktail, Eastern Amberwing, Four-spotted Pennant, Halloween Pennant, Two-striped Forceptail, Orange Bluet, Prince Baskettail

Dragonfly-Friendly Gardening

The Tarn, Acadia National Park, Maine

Species: Chalk-fronted Corporal, Eastern Forktail, Slaty Skimmer, Calico Pennant, Ebony Jewelwing, Four-spotted Skimmer, Dusky Clubtail, Common Green Darner, Frosted Whiteface, Dot-tailed Whiteface

Wyman Park, Baltimore, Maryland

Species: Fragile Forktail, Blue Dasher, Variable Dancer, Common Whitetail, Eastern Pondhawk, Common Green Darner, Ebony Jewelwing, Great Blue Skimmer, Eastern Forktail, Familiar Bluet

Fresh Pond Reservation, Cambridge, Massachusetts

Species: Blue-fronted Dancer, Blue Dasher, Eastern Forktail, Autumn Meadowhawk, Slaty Skimmer, Fragile Forktail, Eastern Pondhawk, Common Whitetail, Black-shouldered Spinyleg, White-faced Meadowhawk

Gallup Park, Ann Arbor, Michigan

Species: Eastern Forktail, Eastern Pondhawk, Blue-fronted Dancer, Fragile Forktail, Widow Skimmer, Eastern Amberwing, Common Whitetail, Orange Bluet, American Rubyspot, Slaty Skimmer

Where to See Dragonflies

Coldwater Spring, Minneapolis, Minnesota

Species: Eastern Forktail, Eastern Pondhawk, Widow Skimmer, Western Red Damsel, Twelve-spotted Skimmer, Blue Dasher, Common Whitetail, Cobra Clubtail, Common Green Darner, Dot-tailed Whiteface

Mississippi Sandhill Crane National Wildlife Refuge, Jackson, Mississippi

Species: Slaty Skimmer, Halloween Pennant, Eastern Pondhawk, Blue Corporal, Blue Dasher, Needham's Skimmer, Golden-winged Skimmer, Banded Pennant, Amanda's Pennant, Little Blue Dragonlet

Rock Bridge Memorial State Park, Columbia, Missouri

Species: Ebony Jewelwing, Widow Skimmer, Eastern Pondhawk, Common Whitetail, Halloween Pennant, Blue-faced Meadowhawk, Blue Dasher, Powdered Dancer, Blue Corporal, Blue-tipped Dancer

Lake McDonald, Glacier National Park, Montana

Species: Pale Snaketail, Paddle-tailed Darner, Emerald Spreadwing, White-faced Meadowhawk, Striped Meadowhawk, Variegated Meadowhawk, Lake Darner, Emma's Dancer, Boreal Bluet, Saffron-winged Meadowhawk

Dragonfly-Friendly Gardening

Holmes Lake Park, Lincoln, Nebraska

Species: Eastern Forktail, Blue Dasher, Twelve-spotted Skimmer, Widow Skimmer, Halloween Pennant, Black Saddlebags, Eastern Amberwing, Eastern Pondhawk, Common Whitetail, Familiar Bluet

Ash Meadows National Wildlife Refuge, Nye County, Nevada

Species: Variegated Meadowhawk, Western Pondhawk, Familiar Bluet, American Rubyspot, Paiute Dancer, Kiowa Dancer, Blue-ringed Dancer, Widow Skimmer, Flame Skimmer, White-belted Ringtail

Heads Pond, Hooksett, New Hampshire

Species: Blue Dasher, Eastern Pondhawk, Chalk-fronted Corporal, Slaty Skimmer, White Corporal, Racket-tailed Emerald, Spangled Skimmer, Sedge Sprite, Meadowhawk, Eastern Amberwing

Cape May Point State Park, New Jersey

Species: Eastern Pondhawk, Familiar bluet, Rambur's Forktail, Blue Dasher, Common Whitetail, Black Saddlebags, Halloween Pennant, Needham's Skimmer, Carolina Saddlebags, Common Green Darner

Where to See Dragonflies

Bitter Lake National Wildlife Refuge, New Mexico

Species: Desert Whitetail, Flame Skimmer, Western Pondhawk, Comanche Skimmer, Variegated Meadowhawk, Familiar Bluet, Aztec Dancer, Blue Dasher, Desert Forktail, Bleached Skimmer

Cornell Botanic Gardens, Ithaca, New York

Species: Eastern Forktail, Stream Bluet, Eastern Amberwing, Powdered Dancer, Variable Dancer, Familiar Bluet, Widow Skimmer, Common Whitetail, Eastern Pondhawk, Ebony Jewelwing

Lake Johnson, Raleigh, North Carolina

Species: Blue-fronted Dancer, Common Whitetail, Blue Dasher, Great Blue Skimmer, Slaty Skimmer, Eastern Amberwing, Widow Skimmer, Halloween Pennant, Fragile Forktail, Ebony Jewelwing

Sheyenne National Grassland, Ransom, North Dakota

Species: Dot-tailed Whiteface, Twelve-spotted Skimmer, Common Green Darner, Horned Clubtail, Taiga Bluet, Common Baskettail, Widow Skimmer, Eastern Pondhawk, Variegated Meadowhawk, Common Whitetail

Dragonfly-Friendly Gardening

Headlands Beach State Park, Mentor, Ohio

Species: Eastern Forktail, Blue Dasher, Slender Spreadwing, Common Green Darner, Black Saddlebags, Azure Bluet, Familiar Bluet, Blue-fronted Dancer, Eastern Pondhawk, Widow Skimmer

Lake Thunderbird Park, Norman, Oklahoma

Species: Blue-fronted Dancer, Powdered Dancer, Familiar Bluet, Common Whitetail, Variegated Meadowhawk, Widow Skimmer, American Rubyspot, Eastern Amberwing, Kiowa Dancer, Blue-ringed Dancer

Oaks Bottom Wildlife Park, Portland, Oregon

Species: Pacific Forktail, Eight-spotted Skimmer, Western Pondhawk, Common Green Darner, Variegated Meadowhawk, Blue-eyed Darner, Widow Skimmer, Tule Bluet, Blue Dasher, Cardinal Meadowhawk

John Heinz National Wildlife Refuge at Tinicum, Philadelphia, Pennsylvania

Species: Fragile Forktail, Blue Dasher, Eastern Pondhawk, Eastern Forktail, Common Whitetail, Autumn Meadowhawk, Blue-fronted Dancer, Familiar Bluet, Eastern Amberwing, Orange Bluet

Where to See Dragonflies

Norman Birds Sanctuary, Rhode Island

Species: Eastern Forktail, Blue Dasher, Eastern Amberwing, Eastern Pondhawk, Black Saddlebags, Common Green Darner, Familiar Bluet, Slender Spreadwing, Widow Skimmer

Huntington Beach State Park, Murrells Inlet, South Carolina

Species: Eastern Pondhawk, Four-spotted Pennant, Needham's Skimmer, Great Blue Skimmer, Blue Dasher, Rambur's Forktail, Common Baskettail, Marl Pennant, Halloween Pennant, Black Saddlebags

Farm Island, Hughes County, South Dakota

Species: Widow Skimmer, Common Whitetail, Twelve-spotted Skimmer, Familiar Bluet, Lyre-tipped Spreadwing, Blue-fronted Dancer, Eastern Pondhawk, Eastern Forktail, Lance-tipped Darner, Tule Bluet

Hendersonville Dog Park, Hendersonville, Tennessee

Species: Blue Dasher, Familiar bluet, Common Green Darner, Common Whitetail, Swift Setwing, Swamp Darner, Fragile Forktail, Halloween Pennant, Black Saddlebags, Eastern Amberwing

Aransas National Wildlife Refuge, Texas

Species: Seaside Dragonlet, Eastern Pondhawk, Blue Dasher, Four-spotted Pennant, Familiar Bluet, Common Green Darner, Needham's Skimmer, Rambur's Forktail, Red-tailed Pennant, Red Saddlebags

Utah Lake State Park, Provo, Utah

Species: Blue Dasher, Variegated Meadowhawk, Striped Meadowhawk, Band-winged Meadowhawk, Common Green Darner, Blue-eyed Darner, Great Spreadwing, Spotted Spreadwing, Twelve-spotted Skimmer, Western Pondhawk

Ricker Pond, Groton, Vermont

Species: Slaty Skimmer, Autumn Meadowhawk, Calico Pennant, Variable Dancer, Chalk-fronted Corporal, Eastern Forktail, Baskettail, Skimming Bluet, Black-shouldered Spinyleg, Slender Spreadwing

Claude Moore Park, Sterling, Virginia

Species: Blue Dasher, Common Whitetail, Familiar Bluet, Slaty Skimmer, Eastern Amberwing, Eastern Pondhawk, Unicorn Clubtail, Fragile Forktail, Widow Skimmer, Twelve-spotted Skimmer

Where to See Dragonflies

Meadowlark Botanical Gardens, Vienna, Virginia

Species: Blue Dasher, Eastern Pondhawk, Slaty Skimmer, Widow Skimmer, Autumn Meadowhawk, Halloween Pennant, Fragile Forktail, Common Whitetail, Eastern Amberwing, Variable Dancer

Mercer Slough Nature Park, Bellevue, Washington

Species: Pacific Forktail, Eight-spotted Skimmer, Cardinal Meadowhawk, Shadow Darner, Western Pondhawk, Tule Bluet, Paddle-tailed Darner, California Darner, Blue-eyed Darner, Autumn Meadowhawk

Washington Park Aboretum, Seattle, Washington

Species: Eight-spotted Skimmer, Blue Dasher, Pacific Forktail, Cardinal Meadowhawk, Common Whitetail, Striped Meadowhawk, Paddle-tailed Darner, Spotted Spreadwing, Shadow Darner, Blue-eyed Darner

Where to See Dragonflies
(elsewhere)

For Europe, we strongly recommend consulting *The Field Guide to the Dragonflies of Britain and Europe*, by Klaas-Douwe B Dijkstra and Richard Lewington, (British Wildlife Publishing, 2020). This highly informative book has excellent illustrations of all European odonata, together with distribution maps for each individual species.

There is also dragonflies.online, a useful, regularly updated website for dragonflies and damselflies in and around Europe.

For all other parts of the world, we recommend the fine online network iNaturalist.org. This website is interactive and it provides a forum for sightings and locations worldwide, for all fauna including dragonflies and damselflies.

How to Support
Dragonfly Conservation

Record dragonflies in your area

Anyone can start recording and documenting the dragonflies they find, and these records can become part of an invaluable data set, used in ensuring the protection of dragonflies for years to come.

The British Dragonfly Society uses iRecord to receive records, and you can easily submit yours to the site online here: british-dragonflies.org. uk/recording/submit-your-records/

The above link also includes a helpful beginners guide to what a record includes and how to make one.

In North America and South America, you can create an account with Odanata Central and record dragonfly and damselfly sightings through their website: www.odonatacentral.org

You can also find hotspots in your area and add to records using the app iNaturalist from anywhere in the world.

Support or volunteer at dragonfly conservation projects

Across the UK, Dragonfly hotspots are looking for volunteers to help with a broad range of tasks, from habitat management to visitor engagement and outreach. This comprehensive list from the Dragonfly Society will guide you to your nearest hotspots and opportunities to volunteer there: british-dragonflies.org.uk/what-we-do/outreach-projects/hotspots-project

In North, Central and South America, you can become a member of the Dragonfly Society of the Americas (DSA). The membership fees go towards the conservation of dragonflies and damselflies across North, Central and South America, and can be joined by people anywhere in the world.

Acknowledgements

I blame this book entirely on my publisher, Sara Hunt. If she hadn't sat gamely through a presentation of my previous book at a literary event in Grantown-on-Spey, it never would have happened. After I'd finally shut up answering a lady about how to make a dragonfly pond in her garden, Sara came up to me and said, 'There's a book in that. If you write it, I'll publish it.' So I did. And she has. I can't thank her enough. It's impossible to imagine a nicer publisher, nor one who could make me laugh so much.

And the book would be no good at all without my wife Kari de Koenigswarter's tremendous contribution. She knows far more about water plants and dragonfly larvae than I do, her illustrations are invaluable, and she has given an enormous amount of time to the project.

As always, I have had terrific help and advice from my loyal writing buddy Frank Woods, and I have been lucky enough once again to have Craig Hillsley as my editor. Just like last time, this book is much better as a result of Craig's thoughtful recommendations and incredible attention to detail. Any residual inaccuracies are entirely mine.

I would also like to acknowledge the debt I owe to Norman Moore, who was my mentor during the creation of Ashton Water Dragonfly Sanctuary, and who, back in the '80s, wrote a basic 'Dig a Pond for Dragonflies', originally issued on A4 sheets by the British Dragonfly Society. This, in an enlarged and more impressive form, is still available from the BDS.

And how to thank the zillions of people with whom I have discussed and learned about ponds over the years, and all the members of the BDS who have been so encouraging? I can't, except to say you are not forgotten!

Also part of the
IN THE MOMENT collection

The Zen of Climbing, Francis Sanzaro

Learn to perfect the art of awareness, of poise amidst chaos.

Climbing is a sport of perception, and our level of attainment is a matter of mind as much as body.

Written by philosopher, essayist, and lifelong climber Francis Sanzaro, *The Zen of Climbing* explores the fundamentals of successful climbing, delving into psychology, neuroscience, philosophy, and Taoism. Awareness, Sanzaro argues, is the alchemy of climbing, allowing us to merge mental and physical attributes in one embodied whole. This compact volume puts the climber's mind at the forefront of practice.

Writing Landscape, Linda Cracknell

Inhabiting a landscape, walking a landscape, writing a place and time

For Linda Cracknell, exposure to wind, rock, mist, and salt water is integral to her writing process. She follows Susan Sontag's advice to "Love words, agonise over sentences, and pay attention to the world," observing and writing her landscapes from the particulars of each moment. In this varied essay collection, Linda backpacks on a small island that is connected to the mainland only at low tide, hikes the wooded hillside close to her home, and retraces a trek made by her parents seven decades earlier. Reading this collection will take you to new places, open your eyes to the world, and suggest ways to take note and make notes as you go—to inspire your own attentive looking, journaling, and writing practice.

Watching Wildlife, Jim Crumley

It is a special privilege and a richly rewarding experience to observe a wild animal hunting, interacting with its young or its mate, exploring its habitat, or escaping a predator.

To watch wildlife, it's essential not only to learn an animal's ways, the times and places you may find it, but also to look inward: to station yourself, focus, and wait.

With decades of close observation of wild animals and birds, Jim Crumley has found himself up close to many of our most elusive creatures, studying their movements, noting details, and offering intimate insights into their extraordinary lives. Here, he draws us into his magical world, showing how we can learn to watch wildlife well, and what doing so can mean for our ability to care for it, and care for ourselves.

Permaculture: Planting the seeds of radical regeneration, Maya Blackwell

Permaculture is a way of farming, gardening, or managing land that emphasises a reciprocal relationship with nature.

Permaculture is also a design process that works with wildness, not against it. And it's an essential resource in the fight of our lives: tackling the climate crisis.

Here, permaculture practitioner and poet Maya Blackwell writes with expertise and personal experience of the transformative power of permaculture for both people and the planet. You will discover how the practice nurtures individual and collective wellbeing. There are opportunities throughout for reflection and connection. Whether you're new to permaculture or someone with years of experience, this book contains tools for growth bringing rewards far beyond the garden.

Atoms of Delight, Kenneth Steven

Poet and essayist Kenneth Steven takes us on a series of meditative quests in search of his "atoms of delight"—treasures, both natural and spiritual—through some of our most beautiful landscapes.

The short pieces in this captivating collection invite readers to accompany Steven as he seeks out crystal-clear waters, an elusive bird, orchids, berries, or pebbles polished by time and tide. Appreciative of the grace of silence and the value of solitude, he takes journeys that prompt introspection and provoke memories as we pause and discover alongside him the transformative power of nature's small gifts and wild places.

This is an evocative book that will inspire you to pay close attention and reflect on the fleeting moments of joy that nature has brought into your life. As you set out on your own pilgrimages, you will discover the extraordinary that can be found in the everyday when you take the time to look for it.

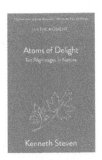

RUARY MACKENZIE DODDS is one of the country's leading experts on dragonflies. His memoir, *The Dragonfly Diaries* (Saraband, 2014), chronicles the ups and downs of establishing Europe's first public dragonfly sanctuary. Ruary is in great demand to share his expertise and enthusiasm with festival, radio and TV audiences, and he often contributes to BBC programmes such as *Countryfile* and *Springwatch*. Ruary now divides his time between Britain and New Zealand and is proud to be called one of the British Dragonfly Society's 'Dragonfly Ambassadors'.

Born in Mexico, KARI DE KOENIGSWATER is an artist who currently divides her time between her home and studios in Edinburgh and New Zealand. Kari inherited her fascination for insects from her grandfather Charles Rothschild, and was encouraged by her aunt Miriam. Dragonflies have featured in her art. She has researched the larval stages of dragonflies and works together with Ruary to promote dragonfly conservation in New Zealand.